FROM BARLEY TO BLARNEY

A Whiskey Lover's Guide to Ireland

Sean Muldoon, *Pub Expert*
Jack McGarry, *Mixed Drink Expert*
Tim Herlihy, *Distillery Expert*

Elaine Hill, *Photographer*
Conor Kelly, *Writer*

Andrews McMeel
PUBLISHING®

"Dedicated to Mum."

Andrews McMeel Publishing
a division of Andrews McMeel Universal
1130 Walnut Street, Kansas City, Missouri 64106

www.andrewsmcmeel.com

19 20 21 22 23 TEN 10 9 8 7 6 5 4 3 2 1

ISBN: 978-1-4494-8993-9

Library of Congress Control Number: 2018953085

Editor: Jean Z. Lucas
Designer: Drinksology
Production Editor: Elizabeth A. Garcia
Production Manager: Carol Coe

All photography by Elaine Hill except for reprinted with permission:

Vern Evans—photos of Jim O' The Mill, page 147
Jeff Harvey—photo of Tullamore Distillery stills, page 46
David Hogan—photos of The Dublin Liberties Distillery stills, pages 86-87
Michael Scully—photo of Clonakilty Distillery stills, page 130
Shannon Sturgis—photo of Irish Coffee, page 259
Cain O'Sullivan—photo of construction worker, page 87

ATTENTION: SCHOOLS AND BUSINESSES
Andrews McMeel books are available at quantity discounts
with bulk purchase for educational, business, or sales
promotional use. For information, please e-mail the
Andrews McMeel Publishing Special Sales Department:
specialsales@amuniversal.com.

The title of this book has a double meaning. It is both for whiskey lovers and by whiskey lovers.

Researching and compiling it has truly been a passion product for the team behind it. We are, first and foremost, evangelists for Irish whiskey, and we're on a mission to spread the word. Welcome to our labor of love.

SLÁINTE!

Poppy pauses to admire Downpatrick Head in County Mayo.

CONTENTS

A Distilled HISTORY of Distillation

The word "whiskey" comes from the Irish uisce beatha, *meaning "water of life." So you can see, we've always cast an earnest eye on the matter.*

A.D. 600-900

Irish monks return from continental Europe with distillation equipment for creating medicines. Ever resourceful, they discover other uses for it.

1405

In the Annals of Clonmacnoise, *the earliest written Irish record of whiskey attributes the demise of a chieftain to "taking a surfeit of aqua vitae (uisce beatha)" at Christmas. Death by water of life: also the earliest known example of Irish irony.*

1608

King James I awards the first license to the Bushmills Distillery in County Antrim. Poitín-makers are unimpressed and carry on.

1700s

First celebrity endorsements: Sir Walter Raleigh, Elizabeth I, and Peter the Great all declare their love of uisce beatha. *Peter goes as far as to say, "Of all wines, Irish wine is best." In our book, that's good enough to be Great, Peter.*

1770s

There are by now some 1,200 distilleries on the island of Ireland. Most have no license because that would mean paying duties to you-know-who . . .

1785

You-know-who impose taxes on malted barley. In response to this brazen move by the English, the Irish begin to distill using malted and unmalted barley—and invent pot still whiskey. So there.

1830

Former taxman Aeneas Coffey invents a still that enables continuous distillation. Irish distillers say, "No thanks. See if the Scots lads want it."

1838

Uh-oh. A national temperance movement is launched. Within five years over half the population has taken The Pledge and given up alcohol. Domestic demand collapses and many distilleries close.

1850s

Aeneas Coffey's invention is doing well with Scottish distillers. Too well.

1879

The four big Dublin distillers (John Jameson, William Jameson, John Powers, and George Roe) publish a rousing pamphlet, Truths about Whisky, *which calls for the banning of "silent spirit"—grain whiskey produced by the Coffey still. Bewilderingly, the pamphlet fails to change the world.*

1890

Phylloxera wipes out pot still's chief competitor, French brandy. Irish distilleries shrug nonchalantly, say "zut alors," and increase output.

1900s

Scottish distilleries see continued growth in blended whisky. The Scottish Distillers Company Limited conglomerate opens its own Irish distillery in Dublin. What nerve, we think. But it's successful, so that's OK.

1909

In defining "whiskey," a Royal Commission approves Scottish-style distilling of silent spirit. It's a huge blow to the Irish industry, which is driven to considering publishing another rousing pamphlet.

1916-1930

Scottish Coffey stills create a surplus and prices collapse. The Irish War of Independence disrupts production and closes off access to key Commonwealth markets such as Canada. In the United States, Prohibition comes into effect in 1920. The party is over.

1933

The end of Prohibition releases pent-up U.S. demand that the now-devastated Irish industry is unable to meet. But the canny Scots can. Grrr.

1943

Bartender Joe Sheridan improvises a new drink at Foynes, the precursor to Shannon Airport. His Irish Coffee effectively ensures that the ailing Irish whiskey industry still has a pulse.

1945

American soldiers return home from the United Kingdom after World War II with a newly acquired taste for Scotch. This further drives up U.S. demand.

1950s-1960s

Scotch flourishes in the United States and becomes a misspelled byword for proper whiskey.

1966

The remaining Irish distillers merge to form Irish Distillers Limited (IDL) and declare "Step aside, kilt-wearers—whiskey coming through!"

1975

IDL takes a gamble and opens a new state-of-the art distillery in Midleton, County Cork. It's the last throw of the dice. IDL's luck is in.

1987

John Teeling converts an old state industrial plant into the Cooley Distillery—effectively ending IDL's monopoly of Irish whiskey production.

1990–2000

Demand returns for all traditional styles of Irish whiskey—pot still, single malt, blended, and single grain. With great magnanimity, we forgive Scotland.

2000–present

For the past twenty years, Irish whiskey has been the fastest-growing spirit in the world. At home, new distilleries are opening—twenty-five to date plus another ten at planning stage. Brands are being launched and old ones revived. We rediscover a taste for innovation with mashbills, distilling techniques, cask maturation, and finishing. Once more, things are looking lively for the water of life.

STYLES OF
IRISH WHISKEY

MALT IRISH WHISKEY

This style of whiskey is 100 percent malted barley and made in a pot still. A single malt is a whiskey made in a single distillery. Examples include Tyrconnell, Knappogue Castle 12-year-old, and Bushmills 21-year-old.

FLAVOR: *Malt whiskey gives you fruit notes such as green apple or orange. Malt can also be peated, such as Connemara, which will have a smokiness to it.*

POT STILL IRISH WHISKEY

Pot still is from malted and unmalted barley and distilled in copper pot stills. This style can also include up to 5 percent other grains, such as oats and rye. This is the classic, even quintessential, style of Irish whiskey. Good current examples are Green Spot and Redbreast.

FLAVOR: *spicy, peppery, and with a pronounced creamy mouthfeel.*

GRAIN IRISH WHISKEY

Made from corn or wheat with a small percentage of malted barley for the enzymes to help convert starch into sugar during the mashing process (at right). Distilled in column stills, grain whiskey is the backbone of Irish blends. It is rarely found on its own, though Teeling and Kilbeggan both produce a single grain whiskey.

FLAVOR: light, sweet, and delicate; often with vanilla notes

BLENDED IRISH WHISKEY

This is a fairly broad term that covers combinations of all of the previous. It's now the most common style of Irish whiskey. Examples include Jameson, Tullamore D.E.W., Powers Gold Label, and Bushmills Original.

FLAVOR: *This varies widely according to the nature of whiskeys involved. As a rule, though, it is smooth and soft on the palate, with a generous finish.*

HOW *IRISH WHISKEY IS MADE*

SHORT ANSWER: *Magic.*
SLIGHTLY LONGER ANSWER:
Water, malted and unmalted barley, yeast.
Fermentation. Distillation. And magic.
EVEN LONGER ANSWER:
Boy, you really won't let this go, will you?
OK THEN . . .

2. MASHING

The malted barley is added to warm water. This creates the "mash." Malted barley can be combined with unmalted barley for a pot still mash, or corn (maize) for grain whiskey.

1. MALTING

We soak barley for a couple of days in warm water. When it begins to sprout, we dry it. This is malting.

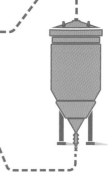

4. DISTILLING

We heat the liquid in copper or column stills until the alcohol vaporizes. This is the good stuff. We then condense the vapors into liquid, collect it, repeat two or three times, and get excited.

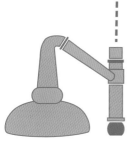

3. FERMENTING

We add yeast and put the mash, now called wort, in a fermentation tank. The yeast converts the sugars to alcohol. This beer-like liquid is the "wash."

5. AGING

We add water to the spirit and put it all in a lovely old cask. We wait for a minimum of three years, then we wait some more.

6. BOTTLING

After an unspecified number of years, we transfer the whiskey from the lovely old cask to a lovely new bottle. And we raise a glass.

AND THAT'S IT.
HAPPY NOW?

THE COUNTRY OF
IRELAND

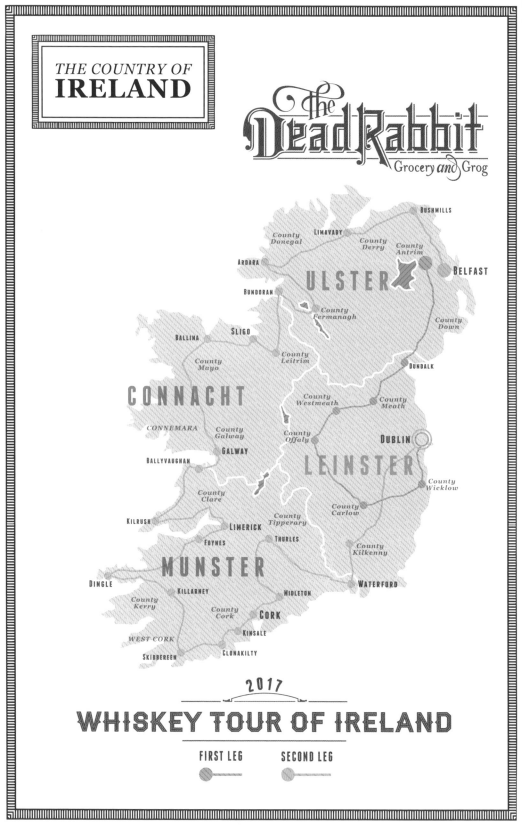

2017

WHISKEY TOUR OF IRELAND

FIRST LEG   SECOND LEG

INTRODUCTION

*"What whiskey will not cure,
there is no cure for."*

Irish proverb

Evidently, Irish whiskey has been paying attention to the old proverb, for it is curing itself. From near-oblivion by around the middle of the last century, it's now the fastest-growing type of whiskey in the world, and the fastest-growing spirit in the United States, period. Many of the old distilleries are in new hands and busier than ever, while every week seems to bring word of another entrant to the world of whiskey. It's a busy, busy business.

Whiskey—or *uisce beatha* in the Irish language—is an essential part of Ireland. We were once the world's largest producer, the envy of all for the sublime quality of our pot still spirit. It has shaped our agriculture; our literature and song; and today, increasingly, our economy. Most of our whiskey exports go to the United States. With that thirst comes another—for a proper understanding of what makes Irish whiskey truly different and worth exploring.

From Barley to Blarney: A Whiskey Lover's Guide to Ireland presents the country through its distilleries and the stories that go with them. In each region we visit, the local whiskey-making heritage is the starting point for everything—for history and anecdote, for tall tales, for oddities and, yes, a jar or two. (We also mention a few non-whiskey-related things to

Poppy outside the hotel in the lovely village of Cushendun in the Glens of Antrim.

do or see in each province. Because, people keep telling us, apparently there's more to life. Hmmm.) We begin with the province of Leinster. Historically, it was very significant, and it's the province where you'll find Dublin, the cynosure of the Irish whiskey-making tradition, home to her great distilleries, and so much more. Dublin gets a section of its own, with a discussion of its particular role in the history and future of Irish distilling and, of course, its frankly astonishing pubs.

From this starting point, our journey follows a ragged clockwise path around the other regions, finishing up where we all began—with the province of Ulster in the north.

Along the way, for the true lover, we also discuss the spectrum of styles, taste, and production methods, and meet some of the personalities reshaping the world of Irish whiskey today. In the back of the book you'll find a glossary that explains some of the language of distilling you'll encounter within these pages, as well as one or two less serious but equally useful terms.

Jack McGarry Sr.: The Navigator.

What Are You Having?

Naturally, Ireland's famous pubs also play a major part in the story. You'll learn why they're as influential for their hospitality as for their hooch, and which ones really are worth a trip—a trip we ourselves made twice. In all we spent over five weeks covering first central and southeast Ireland, and then the rest. (Also, we did it in a restored 1976 Volkswagen Microbus called Poppy. But that's a tale for another day.)

We chose fifty Great Irish Pubs, as we've called them, though we could easily have chosen twice as many, and they'd all have been equally and differently Great. How did we come up with the list? We began pooling our collective knowledge and we asked for recommendations from social media. This produced a roll call of around 160 pubs. Intriguing but not altogether practical. So we began cutting the list down. Hard choices had to be made. Hard, foot-stamping, door-slamming, tantrum-inducing choices. Also, it turned out that some pubs we were interested in visiting weren't that interested in being visited. Oh well. And despite all the foot stamping and door slamming we ended up with a short list that was lamentably far from short. Time for even more hard choices (and their consequences). But eventually we finalized our list and set off. We visited each of the fifty pubs here, sometimes more than once; interviewed and recorded the owners at length; took a lot of photographs; and, more importantly, sampled the hospitality—all in the name of editorial accuracy, you understand.

Louise McGuane of Chapel Gate Irish Whiskey Co. in County Clare heard we were on our way.

We've something else important to mention about the pubs, too. There's an old saying in rural Ireland: "A yard of counter is better than an acre of land." That may once have been the case, when the local spirit grocer—a peculiarly Irish type of all-purpose pub-shop—was the commercial hub of the village or townland. Not anymore. The people running what are often family businesses today are working as hard if not harder than their parents and grandparents, which is saying something. Moreover, they speak of the work in terms of a vocation and say things like "You wouldn't do it if you didn't love it." Many also think of themselves as custodians of a precious artifact rather than owners of a commercial asset. Without exception they have a profound respect for heritage and feel a true sense of responsibility to the pubs and to their customers. The smaller and more rural places in particular are sustained by communities of locals and regulars, whom the owners often view as extensions of their own families. We think that's because the Great Irish Pub is, at heart, a shared experience—an experience that's open to all.

We discovered some extraordinary places while on this journey: ancient pubs, hidden pubs, reborn pubs, haunted pubs—even a truly unforgettable pub that only opens one day a week. We loved them all. We hope you'll seek out some of them and experience for yourself this unique and timeless aspect of Irish culture. Trust us, you'll be glad you did, because that's where you'll find the version of Ireland you've always had in your mind. It's real and it's right here—and here, and here . . .

Signed banknotes from around the world on the wall in Courtney's Bar, Killarney, County Kerry.

THE PROVINCE OF
LEINSTER

THE COUNTIES OF
LEINSTER

Carlow   Louth
Dublin   Meath
Kildare   Offaly
Kilkenny   Westmeath
Laois   Wexford
Longford   Wicklow

VISITING LEINSTER AND DUBLIN CITY

THERE ARE MORE COUNTIES IN LEINSTER THAN ANY OTHER PROVINCE IN IRELAND. WHAT'S MORE, ONE OF THOSE COUNTIES IS DUBLIN— WHICH IS A WORLD OF ITS OWN; POSSIBLY SEVERAL. SO ALREADY YOU HAVE A DILEMMA: HOW ARE YOU GOING TO FIT IT ALL IN?

L et's start with the fair city herself. Dublin offers everything any major modern European capital city does: art, culture (high and low), architecture, history, literature, entertainment, shopping, nightlife— the lot. And it does all that with a bit of a swagger and panache. If you can't enjoy Dublin, you may unfortunately have been born to the wrong species. It's the only rational explanation. The new city, with its gleaming citadels of glass and steel, sits comfortably alongside old Dublin—what most of us think of as real Dublin—with its cobbles and street markets. And of course, its pubs. Key sights are Trinity College and the *Book of Kells,* Merrion Square, and the National Gallery (be sure to see the Jack Yeats and Louis le Brocquy paintings). Take a stroll around Temple Bar. It's busy but worth it. Grafton Street is prime retail territory, with lots of interesting side streets to explore.

Muiredach's High Cross—the largest Celtic cross in Ireland, in Monasterboice, County Louth.

Older than the pyramids: the mysterious Neolithic Newgrange in County Meath.

If you never got around to finishing *Ulysses*—first of all, shame on you—try it again while you're here. There are lots of James Joyce trails in the city, as well as events and readings going on all the time, which will help bring the whole wondrous thing to life.

From the buzz of Dublin, head south into beautiful, peaceful County Wicklow. The landscape is lush here, which is why it's known as the Garden of Ireland. There are many walking trails, empty beaches, and historic sites such as the heart-stoppingly lovely Glendalough.

Keep going south and you'll reach Wexford, which was once a Viking settlement (yes, they were here, too). Irish history buffs will enjoy discovering the central role this vibrant, friendly town played in so many key events. Wexford is also home to an internationally renowned opera festival every October.

If you're looking for a different kind of entertainment, look northwest to Kilkenny—chances are, you'll find some kind of festival going on. Whether it's arts, comedy, theater, or music, they do enjoy a get-together there all year round. Why not join them? You'll be most welcome.

Glendalough: One of the most famously beautiful places in Ireland.

A SHORT HISTORY OF
DISTILLING IN LEINSTER

Many countries are really two countries: There's the capital (with its hinterland) and then everything else. In France, for example, there is Paris and then there is what is described as *en province*, i.e., not-Paris. We've a little of that in Ireland, too: There's Dublin and not-Dublin.

Our capital city is a hefty presence, as it should be. That presence, and the rest of the accompanying county (also conveniently called Dublin), is in the province of Leinster. The story of Dublin distilling is long and engrossing. It was, after all, the center of the whiskey-making world for the best part of a century. That has tended to skew the tale of the rest of the province. But a lot of whiskey has also been distilled in not-Dublin, going all the way back to the arrival of the medieval monks with their alembics. One of the first written records of *uisce beatha* in Ireland speaks of Drogheda, in County Meath. Ireland's oldest licensed distillery is the legendary Kilbeggan, in County Westmeath. And Leinster is also home to not one but two of the distilleries that have been instrumental in the resuscitation of the once-moribund whiskey industry: Great Northern and Cooley. What's more, these are connected by the same figure, the charismatic John Teeling.

With Cooley, Teeling brought back to life several long-vanished Kilbeggan brands. And with Great Northern, he has created a large contract distiller able to produce grain, double- and triple-distilled malt, and pot still whiskeys. These, among other things, constitute the new-make spirit many of the start-up distilleries need. And so the wheel turns.

Numerous interesting newer producers, such as Boann and Walsh, have set up in Leinster. The beautiful Powerscourt Estate down in Wicklow now has an impressive-looking distillery under way, as does the equally historic Slane Castle Estate. The latter is backed by the giant Brown-Forman group, owner of Jack Daniels.

When it comes to the story of Irish whiskey-making, of the four provinces of Ireland, Leinster is perhaps the trouble child—the one that has given the most heartache. It's the one that promised so much, delivered so much, and lost so much. Every crazy twist in the tale has been played out here and writ large for the world to see. Its soaring heights were the highest and its plummeting lows the lowest. But Leinster's recovery contains several of the most vital moving parts of the engine driving Irish whiskey today. We couldn't have got to this point without it. And, to a large extent, what happens in Leinster will determine where we go from here.

LEINSTER
DISTILLERIES OF TODAY

*In Leinster, there's more
to distilling than Dublin.
A lot more.*

GRAIN
1605-218

no		nos
~~2975~~	—	~~195~~
2976	—	194
2977	ABV	198
2978	—	198
2979	—	194
2980	—.	196

COOLEY DISTILLERY

IT NEVER WAS MUCH TO LOOK AT IT. THEN AGAIN, THE OLD CEIMICI TEORANTA PLANT OUTSIDE DUNDALK WAS NEVER IN IT FOR THE GLAMOUR. IT WAS ONE OF A NUMBER OF FACILITIES BUILT BY THE IRISH STATE YEARS AGO TO PRODUCE INDUSTRIAL ALCOHOL AND NEUTRAL SPIRIT FOR THE CHEMICAL AND PHARMACEUTICAL SECTORS. BY 1987 IT HAD BEEN CLOSED FOR SOME TIME AND LOOKED LIKELY TO STAY THAT WAY. AFTER ALL, WHO WOULD WANT IT?

Riverstown
Cooley
County Louth

www.cooleywhiskey.com

THE PROVINCE OF
LEINSTER

J ohn Teeling would. He'd been quietly working on a plan to kick-start the independent spirit of Irish distilling, which for years had been largely concentrated in the hands of a few multinational groups. The Dundalk operation—which he renamed Cooley—offered the ideal setting to put the plan into action. When he refitted the plant as a whiskey distillery, it was the first new one built in Ireland in over a century, and it broke the de facto monopoly the Irish Distillers Group had held since the 1970s. Within ten years of opening, Cooley won a major international quality award: a first for an Irish distillery.

Right from the start, Cooley was a place of true innovation. An early indication of the subversiveness to come was when Teeling rejected the received wisdom that triple-distillation was the only game in town, as far as Irish whiskey was concerned.

Oh, if barrels could talk . . .

Instead, he adopted the Scotch model of double-distilling in copper pot stills (which he sourced from the long-closed Old Comber distillery in County Down). He also had the plant's original industrial column stills refurbished to produce grain whiskey for blending. What was he doing with all this product? Selling it as sourced whiskey to retailers as private-label whiskey and to other distilleries, especially to the new kids on the block.

Once Cooley was operational, the next and main phase of Teeling's plan could go into effect: reviving once-forgotten brands such as Locke's, Tyrconnell, Kilbeggan, and— controversially—a peated single malt, Connemara, which was seen as an attempt to take on the more popular style of Scotch. If it was a gamble, it was a good one. (As Teeling memorably said, "Risk isn't a philosophy, it's an addiction.") Since its launch in the 1990s, Connemara has successfully proved Teeling's instincts correct, and the distillery's revival of historic lines has demonstrated a profound understanding of the traditions of Irish whiskey-making. In a further break with convention, Cooley also opted to bottle a single grain, Greenore. This has since been rebranded as Kilbeggan Single Grain and continues to be a very popular addition to the range.

AT A GLANCE

FIRST DISTILLATION
1989

STILLS
*2 Pot Stills (Wash Still: 16,000L,
Spirit Still: 16,000L)
3 Column Stills*

LPA
4 million

WHISKEY STYLES
*Single Malt, Pot Still,
& Grain. Plus Peated*

VISITOR CENTER/TOURS
No

KEY BOTTLINGS

TYRCONNELL SINGLE MALT
*ABV: 40%; also port, sherry,
and Madeira finishes, all
ABV: 46%*

CONNEMARA PEATED SINGLE MALT
ABV: 40%

KILBEGGAN BLENDED
ABV: 40%

KILBEGGAN SINGLE GRAIN
ABV: 43%

LOCKE'S SINGLE MALT
ABV: 40%

All Cooley maturation—which,
except for special finishes, is done
exclusively in ex-bourbon barrels—
takes place on-site at Cooley and
at the Kilbeggan distillery in
County Westmeath.

In 2012 Cooley was acquired by
Beam International and is now part
of the global Beam Suntory group.
And the Teeling family's subversive
instinct has moved on. After Cooley,
John founded Great Northern—
Ireland's largest independent
distillery—nearby in Dundalk, while
sons Jack and Stephen opened their
own award-winning operation in
Dublin, the first new distillery in the
capital in 125 years.

Cooley may have begun in
inauspicious surroundings, but its
history and legacy have been key
factors in shaping Irish distilling
today.

GREAT NORTHERN DISTILLERY

THERE'S A LOT OF ROMANCE IN WHISKEY; POETRY EVEN. NO DOUBT IT HAS SOMETHING TO DO WITH THE PASSION INVOLVED IN IT—AND OH, THE WAITING, THE WAITING . . . THERE'S SOMETHING AKIN TO LONGING THERE. AND THE WORD ITSELF EVEN SOUNDS A BIT WISTFUL.

Carrick Road
Dundalk
County Louth

www.gndireland.com

THE PROVINCE OF
LEINSTER

Combine that with the quasi-mystical alchemical nature of the process, the coaxing of an extraordinary thing from the most commonplace ingredients: grain, yeast, water. The art of blending and the unquantifiable magic can all make even the hardiest souls grow a little misty-eyed.

But not here. For this is not art but commerce. And that's no bad thing.

Established in 2015, Great Northern Distillery is today Ireland's largest independent distillery—by quite some margin—producing three styles of whiskey: malt, grain, and pot still. It was originally built for volume, as a former Diageo brewery producing Guinness and ale, and subsequently converted solely to make Harp lager. They run both pot stills and column stills here, and make grain, double- and triple-distilled malt, peated malt, and pot still whiskey.

Unsurprisingly, there's no visitor center here. But we're featuring Great Northern because of its central

Great Northern: It's not art, it's commerce.

importance to Irish whiskey-making today. Its key market is private labels and contract distilling, with some retail own-label production, though the distillery has actually recently released its first own bottling—Burke's Irish Whiskey, an exclusive, cask-strength single malt.

Great Northern also provides stocks for smaller distilleries. So, for example, when a brand-new distillery business is launched fully equipped with maturing whiskey stocks, that's one possible explanation of where the stocks came from. There are few sources of new-make spirit in Ireland: The pot stills and column stills here are two of them. As a contract producer, Great Northern will provide your shiny new distillery with new (or aged) spirit to your requested standard and profile. It's a sort of bespoke whiskey tailoring service. They can even provide casks. Or just bring your own along and they'll fill them for you.

Great Northern is headed by the maverick, engaging, and teetotal John Teeling . . .

Great Northern is headed by the maverick, engaging, and teetotal John Teeling, something of a titan of modern Irish distilling. He is the man behind the transformation of the Cooley Distillery and the revival of iconic, long-lost brands such as Kilbeggan and Tyrconnell. (His sons run the new and award-winning Teeling Distillery in Dublin. In fact, the family involvement in the business goes back as far as the eighteenth century.) John Teeling has been a central character in many of the key developments of Irish whiskey over the past thirty years or so. He's seen it all, and has few illusions. "We're now seen as visionaries. We used to be seen as eejits." (He didn't actually say eejits, but you get the picture.)

There may be no illusions about whiskey distilling here, but there is no philistinism either. There are depths of knowledge and experience in Great Northern that few can match anywhere. There is an in-house laboratory that monitors quality and models the spirit profiles for clients. The equipment is state-of-the-art. The commitment to quality is unwavering and borders on the obsessive. Today, just like every day, at Great Northern they will go about the business of producing the finest spirits they can possibly make. As for the poetry, they'll leave that to others.

Some of the busiest fermenters in Ireland.

The dean of distillation:
John Teeling,
still talking whiskey.

AT A GLANCE

FIRST DISTILLATION
2015

STILLS
3 Pot Stills (Wash Still: 50,000L,
Intermediate Still: 26,000L,
Spirit Still: 26,000L)
3 Column Stills

LPA
16 million

WHISKEY STYLES
Single Malt, Pot Still,
& Grain. Plus Peated

VISITOR CENTER/TOURS
No

KEY BOTTLINGS

BURKE'S 14-YEAR-OLD SINGLE MALT
ABV: 59%

A mash tun and
a lauter tun.

BOANN DISTILLERY

IN THE HISTORY OF IRISH WHISKEY, DROGHEDA HOLDS A PARTICULARLY IMPORTANT PLACE. IN FACT, SEVERAL OF THEM. ONE OF THE FIRST WRITTEN RECORDS OF THE SPIRIT IN IRELAND REFERENCES THE TOWN. BY THE LATE EIGHTEENTH CENTURY, THERE WERE NEARLY TWENTY DISTILLERIES HERE ALONE. A HUNDRED YEARS ON, ONE OF THESE WAS, BY QUITE SOME MEASURE, AMONG THOSE PRODUCING THE GREATEST VOLUME OF WHISKEY IN IRELAND.

Platin Road
Drogheda
County Meath

www.boanndistillery.ie

THE PROVINCE OF
LEINSTER

Ａnd there's one other interesting footnote. In 1812 a young inspector for Excises and Taxes began working here, studying the work of distilleries. His name was Aeneas Coffey. Evidently, he learned well.

When Boann Distillery becomes fully operational, its whiskey will be the first produced in Drogheda in over fifty years. It will be the work of the Cooney family—Pat and his wife, Marie, their daughters, Sally-Anne and Celestine, and sons, James, Peter, and Patrick Jr. They're all involved in the venture. And there's a lot of expertise in that team. Pat senior is a veteran of the Irish drinks industry, having spent decades building up what was a small bottling concern into Gleeson Group, a major drinks branding and distribution business. The family's holding company, Na Cuana, also includes Boyne Brewhouse, Adam Cidery, and Merrys Irish Cream Liqueur.

Pat Cooney is an exceptionally fine whistler. And whiskey-maker. Put the two together and . . .

The stunning fifty thousand-square-foot building (which was once a car showroom) opened in 2016. It already houses a craft brewery and taproom, with plans for a restaurant, visitor center, and gift shop. The brewery is operating, creating a range of beers, as well as ciders with apples from the company's own orchards. (In time those orchards may also produce a Calvados.)

The heart of any whiskey distillery is of course the stills. Boann's are high-tech, handmade copper stills with reflux control coils in the neck. As a result, the theory goes, the spirit is exposed to more copper than in a standard pot still.

John McDougall, famously the only man to have distilled all five types of Scotch whisky (single malt, blended malt, single grain, blended, and blended grain), as well as Irish, is a consultant for Boann. A former pupil of his, Aine O'Hora, is the resident distiller.

Pat Cooney,
whiskey-maker
and whistler.

The distillery has a mission to be 100 percent natural and 100 percent Irish. The water comes from Boann's own well and is part of a closed-loop recycling and heat recovery system that also feeds the packaging lines and the restaurant. In due course it will also supply the visitor center and offices. Rainwater is harvested and used to cultivate gin botanicals. (They have plans here for a hedgerow gin and another with a cider base.) All by-products—the pot ale and spent grains, etc.—are returned to the local economy as animal food.

The family's own extensive wine cellars have put at the distillery's disposal an unusually wide range of casks— including, of course, bourbon, sherry, rum, and port, but also Burgundy, Bordeaux, Sauternes, Tokay, Madeira, and Marsala.

Boann, the river goddess, is back in business.

There is sourced whiskey maturing in these barrels at the moment. At the time of our visit, the distillery had some 250 barrels of grain and 200 of malt whiskey aging in oloroso casks in their warehouse in Clonmel.

The heart of any whiskey distillery is of course the stills . . .

The setup at Boann is no artisan, cottage-industry arrangement. It is technically impressive and well-considered. It happens to have impressive views, as well.

According to Celtic mythology, Boann was the goddess of the River Boyne, around which the town of Drogheda grew. She's been quiet for a long time. But rumor has it, she's coming back, and in quite some style.

AT A GLANCE

FIRST DISTILLATION
2018

STILLS
3 Pot Stills (Sunshine: 10,000L, Sally: 7,500L, Celestine: 5,000L)

LPA
250,000

WHISKEY STYLES
Single Pot Still

VISITOR CENTER/TOURS
Yes

KEY BOTTLINGS

THE WHISTLER 7-YEAR-OLD BLUE NOTE SINGLE MALT,
ABV: 46%

THE WHISTLER 10-YEAR SINGLE MALT,
ABV: 46%

SLANE WHISKEY DISTILLERY

HISTORY IS EVERYWHERE HERE. SLANE DISTILLERY IS LOCATED WITHIN THE VAST SLANE CASTLE ESTATE—SOME 1,500 ACRES OF GROUNDS, GARDENS, FOREST, AND FARMLAND IN THE ANCIENT BOYNE VALLEY.

Slane Castle Demesne
Slane
County Meath

www.slaneirishwhiskey.com

THE PROVINCE OF
LEINSTER

The castle itself is cradled in a natural amphitheater, which has provided the backdrop for huge rock concerts featuring everyone from the Rolling Stones, Bob Dylan, and Bruce Springsteen to David Bowie, U2, and Guns N' Roses—all courtesy of the dashing Lord Henry Mount Charles, the 8th Marquess Conyngham.

The distillery is a joint venture between the Conyngham family, which has owned the estate for over three hundred years, and the Kentucky-based Brown-Forman spirits group, owner of Jack Daniels. Cofounder Alex Conyngham, son of Lord Henry, is overseeing the completion of the distillery, which has been designed to be a near-zero-waste enterprise. There is an anaerobic digester—heat and water are recycled, and any organic by-products are returned as animal feed, etc.

At the time of our visit, the distillery was still under construction in the castle's 250-year-old former stable block. When completed, the facility will comprise what is known as a heritage room, highlighting the history of the estate and the region;

Slane's stills look as though they sprouted through the floor of the old stable block.

Yes, it's really a castle.

the barley store; the cooperage; the warehouse; and, of course, the stills. Maturation is currently managed off-site but will move to the distillery when the site is fully operational. Most of the barley for the distillery will be sourced from the Slane estate.

New-make spirit has already been laid down according to Slane's recipe and profile, and is being aged in three different cask types. The Brown-Forman cooperage has supplied virgin and seasoned bourbon barrels, while oloroso sherry casks have been sourced from Jerez, Spain. It's said that the virgin wood, which has a medium char, contributes toasted oak and vanilla to the profile. The bourbon barrels lend a caramel-butterscotch sweetness, while the sherry casks offer dried fruits and spice notes.

The whiskey is presented in a distinctive black bottle. (This is a reference to the old stable block itself. When the restoration work began, the foundations were discovered to contain a lot of black glass dating back several hundred years.)

Slane is Brown-Forman's first venture into Irish whiskey, and the first distillery it has built outside of the United States. The group has invested substantially in the project—a clear indication of both commitment and viability. For this is no artisan, boutique venture. Slane Distillery may be starting small, but it is aiming very high indeed.

The spirit safe: crucial for assessing the distillate coming from the still.

Three of Slane's six column stills.

AT A GLANCE

FIRST DISTILLATION
2018

STILLS
3 Pot Stills (Wash Still: 13,000L, Intermediate Still: 13,000L, Spirit Still: 6,000L)
6 Column Stills

LPA
1.4 million

WHISKEY STYLES
Single Malt, Pot Still & Grain Whiskey

VISITOR CENTER/TOURS
Yes

KEY BOTTLINGS

SLANE BLENDED IRISH WHISKEY
ABV: 40%

POWERSCOURT DISTILLERY

FROM ITS STUNNING SETTING IN THE WICKLOW MOUNTAINS TO THE SCALE OF ITS AMBITION, EVERYTHING ABOUT POWERSCOURT DISTILLERY IS CAPITAL-G GRAND.

Powerscourt Demesne
Enniskerry
County Wicklow

www.powerscourtdistillery.com

THE PROVINCE OF
LEINSTER

Powerscourt: a distillery with spectacular grounds attached or spectacular grounds with a distillery attached? Both.

Still under construction at the time of our visit, the distillery is a joint venture with the historic Powerscourt Estate, which itself attracts over half a million visitors a year to its grounds, castle, and beautiful gardens. The estate has set aside 120 acres of premium barley to supply the distillery. The pure water source is on-site, too.

The home of the distillery will be the estate's old Mill House, which is being restored and extended. It is a substantial building with a large old bell outside that was once used to summon workers from the fields. The site will also house a visitor center, a bar, and a café. Several levels of tour will be offered, from general to a fully immersive VIP experience. Four years in the making, Powerscourt Distillery is the brainchild of financiers Gerry Ginty and Ashley Gardiner, and Sarah Slazenger, managing director of the Powerscourt Estate.

The goal for this field-to-glass venture, says Gerry Ginty, can be expressed in two key attributes: "Authenticity and taste. With certified mineral water from the estate and barley grown on the estate, we are working to create something extra special—the ultimate Irish whiskey." A capital-G Grand Ambition indeed. And the signs are already encouraging.

Fanboy Tim and master distiller Noel Sweeney.

The master distiller here is the award-winning (and Whisky Hall of Famer) Noel Sweeney, formerly head blender at Cooley. The first release is actually sourced whiskey produced by Noel himself during his time at Cooley. The distillery has decided that, when the time is right, it will release its first expressions—two rare single malts, a ten-year-old and a fourteen-year-old—under the brand of Fercullen, which is the ancient name for the townland on which the modern-day Powerscourt Estate sits. It will be the first artisan pot still whiskey produced in Wicklow since the eighteenth century. Currently working on additional profiles and experimenting with finishes—including Madeira, port, sherry, and rum—Noel will oversee all aspects of spirit production and whiskey maturation at the distillery. One thing the estate is not short of is space, so warehousing also will be handled on-site.

Given its remarkable location, Powerscourt can reasonably expect to figure prominently in the burgeoning Irish whiskey tourism industry. The distillery will also be contributing to the rural economy in this part of County Wicklow—and, of course, producing very interesting Irish whiskeys, too. The skills and the pedigree are there. All it needs is what whiskey always demands: time. We recommend you give it some of yours.

From field to glass: The journey starts here.

AT A GLANCE

FIRST DISTILLATION
2018

STILLS
3 Pot Stills (Wash Still: 13,000L, Intermediate Still: 8,500L, Spirit Still: 6,000L)

LPA
800,000 projected

WHISKEY STYLES
Single Malt & Pot Still

VISITOR CENTER/TOURS
Yes

KEY BOTTLINGS

FERCULLEN 10-YEAR-OLD SINGLE MALT

FERCULLEN 14-YEAR-OLD SINGLE MALT

Powerscourt's three pot stills by Forsyths.

KILBEGGAN DISTILLERY

WHAT WAS HAPPENING IN THE WORLD BACK IN 1757? HISTORY, MOSTLY. WILLIAM BLAKE WAS BORN. PAUL REVERE GOT MARRIED. AND IN KILBEGGAN THEY WERE MAKING WHISKEY. THEY STILL ARE. HOWEVER, LIFE HERE IN IRELAND'S OLDEST LICENSED DISTILLERY HAS NOT ALWAYS GONE SMOOTHLY SINCE THE EIGHTEENTH CENTURY. INDEED, QUITE FAR FROM IT.

Lower Main Street
Kilbeggan
County Westmeath
www.kilbeggandistillery.com

THE PROVINCE OF
LEINSTER

Finding Ireland's oldest licensed distillery: If you can read the stack, you're there.

The story is a saga of ambition, revolution, scandal, failure, hope, rebirth—and above all, families.

The McManuses started it all. Their new distillery had everything going for it: water from the River Brosna, grain from local farms, and turf from the surrounding bogland to power the stills. Things went well, but by the turn of the century, the distillery had changed hands. The Codd family invested in it and capitalized on the newly opened Grand Canal to unload materials and move stock more efficiently than before. The distillery prospered and the reputation of its premium pot still whiskeys grew. Then a temperance movement took hold and swept the nation. The distillery declined, but its assets were bought by yet another family, the Lockes, in the mid-1840s. They revived the business and began exporting to England and the United States. The strategy worked—until a perfect storm of disasters arrived in the early half of the twentieth century. Prohibition in the United States, a world war, the Irish War of Independence, trade war with Britain, and then another world war effectively killed off not just Kilbeggan but practically the entire Irish distilling industry. In the aftermath, the Locke family remained nominally in charge, but by 1957 they'd had enough and gave up the fight.

In 2007, some 250 years after it first started, Killbeggan started to distill again . . .

For the next thirty years the distillery lay silent. During that time, it served various functions, including a pig farm, an engineering plant, and a warehouse. But—and this is crucial—the license to distill never expired, thanks to the local community, who kept it up-to-date. In the early 1980s that same community restored the distillery as a whiskey museum. In 1987 yet another family—the Teelings, who had just set up Cooley Distillery—acquired the Kilbeggan license, took over the museum, and built a new distillery on the site. In 2007, some 250 years after it first started, Killbeggan started to distill again, using a 170-year-old still from the old Tullamore distillery.

And in a sense, it was as if nothing much had changed. The same traditional methods, mashing in oak tuns, fermenting in pine vats and original oak vats, even a pot still from over a century and a half ago—all were put to use again. John Teeling helped revive some of the distillery's iconic brands and created the Kilbeggan brand for the German market. A new chapter began; accolades began to arrive, and they have kept arriving. Kilbeggan Distilling Company is now the most-awarded Irish distiller ever. The vast maturation warehouse began to fill up.

In 2012, the global Beam Suntory group bought Kilbeggan. This has helped bring the whiskeys of this historic distillery to a worldwide audience. The visitor experience at Kilbeggan is exceptional, from the restored waterwheel that once powered the entire site, to the stills and the tasting. It is a place that is utterly authentic, proud of its past—and equally optimistic about its future.

Double-distillation: The still on the right is 170 years old.

AT A GLANCE

FIRST DISTILLATION
1757 & 2007

STILLS
2 Pot Stills (Wash Still 3,000L, Spirit Still: 1,800L)

LPA
Less than 100,000

WHISKEY STYLES
Single Malt & Pot Still

VISITOR CENTER/TOURS
Yes

KEY BOTTLINGS

KILBEGGAN DISTILLERY RESERVE SINGLE MALT
ABV: 40%

Wheels within wheels within wheels . . .

TULLAMORE DISTILLERY

WHEN IT COMES TO TULLAMORE, THERE'S DEFINITELY SOMETHING SPECIAL ABOUT THE NUMBER THREE: TRIPLE-DISTILLED, TRIPLE-BLEND, TRIPLE-MATURED. AND OF COURSE, THAT TRIPLE-LETTER SUFFIX: D.E.W.—FOR DANIEL EDMUND WILLIAMS.

Clonminch
Tullamore
County Offaly

www.tullamoredew.com

THE PROVINCE OF
LEINSTER

By the time you've finished counting all the barrels, some of the whiskey in them will be mature.

Williams started work at the distillery in 1862 as a stable boy when he was just fourteen, ending his career sixty years later as owner. In 1893 Tullamore D.E.W. became the name of the original pot still whiskey the distillery produced (along with the enduring slogan "Give every man his D.E.W."). Williams's influence on the business was now so significant that every bottle bore his imprint.

Daniel Williams expanded the Tullamore site and brought in electricity long before its use was widespread across the country. He introduced motor vehicles and ensured the company made use of the new Grand Canal, which would eventually link Dublin with the River Shannon by way of Tullamore. The canal brought in the coal to power the stills, and took away shipments of whiskey for distribution. When Ireland's railway system reached the town, Williams saw to it that the distillery had its own siding.

Under Williams the business prospered, but by the time he died in 1921, Tullamore was about to enter the prolonged decline suffered by most of the Irish distilling industry in the first half of the twentieth century. In 1954 the distillery ceased production. In the mid-1960s the Williams family married into another great Irish distilling dynasty,

the Powers family, with the wedding in Dublin of Teresa Williams to Frank O'Reilly, great-grandson of John Power.

The Tullamore brand became part of Irish Distillers, with production of whiskey shifting from John's Lane in Dublin to Midleton in County Cork. The name was bought by the C&C group in 1994, then sold again, in 2010, to William Grant & Sons, who decided to build a new distillery back where it all began, in Tullamore—returning distilling to the site for the first time in over sixty years.

The symbol of the distillery, a phoenix rising, was seen once again. Production started in 2014—following the same methods as always. Before new-make spirit started to flow in Tullamore, grain and pot still whiskey were sourced at Midleton, with malt produced at Bushmills. All production is now fully grain-to-glass and in-house. There are four mighty warehouses, each holding fifty-five thousand casks.

The old bonded warehouse on-site houses a state-of-the-art visitor center that takes you through not just how Tullamore D.E.W. is made but the remarkable history of the distillery and many of its characters. There are three levels of experience available, from the general introductory to a whiskey master class up to the ultimate, which lasts for almost five hours and includes a behind-the-scenes tour, tasting, lunch, and even a chance to create your own blend.

The secret room where they grow the stills . . .

Three column stills, which also constitute Tullamore town's only skyscraper.

Today, Tullamore D.E.W. is the second-largest-selling Irish whiskey in the world (after Jameson). The style is distinctive, even unique. The range has been extended in recent years to include numerous reserve releases and some experimental cask finishes. Although the relative newness of the distillery places Tullamore in the category of the second wave of Irish whiskey-makers, in truth, it belongs to the great tradition. The address may have changed a couple of times, but Tullamore D.E.W. is finally home again and home to stay. Which, in this triple-obsessed setting, leaves only one more thing to add: three cheers.

AT A GLANCE

FIRST DISTILLATION
2014

STILLS
6 Pot Stills (Pot Wash Still: 21,000L, Malt Wash Still: 16,000L, Two Intermediate Stills: 11,000L, Two Spirit Stills 11,000L) 3 Column Stills

LPA
12.8 million

WHISKEY STYLES
Single Malt, Pot Still & Grain

VISITOR CENTER/TOURS
Yes

KEY BOTTLINGS

The Tullamore range now includes single malt and blended whiskeys—all triple-distilled, of course.

TULLAMORE D.E.W. ORIGINAL
ABV: 40%

12-YEAR-OLD SPECIAL RESERVE
ABV: 40%

15-YEAR-OLD TRILOGY
ABV: 40%

OLD BONDED WAREHOUSE RELEASE
ABV:46%

CIDER CASK FINISH
ABV: 40%

XO RUM CASK FINISH
ABV: 43%

SINGLE MALT 14-YEAR-OLD
ABV: 41.3%

SINGLE MALT 18-YEAR-OLD
ABV: 41.3%

WALSH WHISKEY DISTILLERY

BERNARD WALSH IS A GREAT MAN FOR THE DETAILS.
DETAILS SUCH AS FINDING THE PERFECT LOCATION FOR YOUR
DISTILLERY. UNDERSTANDING THE PROCESSES THAT FAVOR
THE SKILLED HAND OF THE MAKER RATHER THAN THE MIND
OF THE MACHINE. CREATING A VISITOR EXPERIENCE FOR THE
CASUAL VISITOR AS WELL THE SERIOUS AFICIONADO. BERNARD
IS SURROUNDED BY SUCH DETAILS IN ROYAL OAK, HERE IN THE
HEART OF THE HEART OF BARLEY COUNTRY.

Royal Oak
County Carlow

www.walshwhiskey.com

THE PROVINCE OF
LEINSTER

Looks peaceful, doesn't it? And it is.

The distillery, the first to be opened in Carlow in over two hundred years, is today one of the largest independent producers in Ireland, employing around a dozen distillers alone. It's also the first Irish distillery to produce all three core styles of Irish whiskey in the same stillhouse—pot still, malt, and grain. Many of the processes continue to be done by hand, in the traditional nineteenth-century style. Because, Bernard believes, this allows the distiller greater control, especially when making small batches or special runs. The water source is a local aquifer, some seventy feet beneath the fields. All of the distillery's barley is Irish.

Walsh produces two whiskey brands, both triple-distilled, both quite exclusive. The Irishman is traditional in style, a 70/30 blend of single malt and single pot still. When it was launched, it was the only Irish blend containing 100 percent copper pot still distillates and 0 percent grain or column still whiskey.

Writers' Tears is a more modern take on traditional Irish whiskey, in a 60/40 blend of single malt and pot still. Both ranges have won numerous awards worldwide.

Bernard Walsh talking details.

Bernard's journey into whiskey began when his enterprising wife, Rosemary, created a ready-made Irish Coffee drink (the cheekily named Hot Irishman). The product took off, and Bernard undertook to source whiskey to keep up with demand. A task became an interest, which became a passion and eventually a desire to distill his own whiskey.

The focus of the business isn't volume; it's quality—first and last. "We're not looking over our shoulders," says Bernard. "We're looking down the road. And we feel we're just getting going." He believes that the same outlook can be applied to Irish whiskey in general. The industry is, he thinks, at a juncture. And the future will belong neither to heritage nor innovation alone but to quality.

In addition to driving ahead the continued development of the distillery, Bernard Walsh is restoring Holloden House, a Georgian mansion on the Royal Oak estate dating from 1755. He is doing it slowly, brick by numbered brick. That's attention to detail. That's the Walsh way.

A family of pot stills in their native Carlow habitat.

Making the cut: the spirit safe in use.

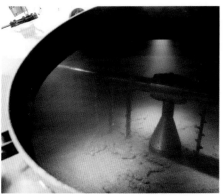

AT A GLANCE

FIRST DISTILLATION
2016

STILLS
*3 Pot stills (Wash Still: 15,000L,
Intermediate Still: 7,500L,
Spirit Still: 10,000L)
2 Column Stills*

LPA
2.5 million

WHISKEY STYLES
Single Malt, Pot Still & Grain

VISITOR CENTER/TOURS
Yes

KEY BOTTLINGS

THE IRISHMAN FOUNDER'S RESERVE
ABV: 40%

THE IRISHMAN 12-YEAR-OLD SINGLE MALT
ABV: 43%

THE IRISHMAN 17-YEAR-OLD
ABV: 56%

WRITERS' TEARS RANGE:

COPPER POT
ABV: 40%

RED HEAD
ABV: 46%

CASK STRENGTH
ABV: 53%

BALLYKEEFE DISTILLERY

FARMERS ARE A RESOURCEFUL, RESILIENT LOT. WHERE OBSTACLES EXIST, THEY FIND A WAY AROUND THEM. WHERE NO OPPORTUNITIES EXIST, SOMETIMES THEY CREATE THEM.

Kyle
Cuffesgrange
County Kilkenny

www.ballykeefedistillery.ie

THE PROVINCE OF
LEINSTER

Take Morgan Ging, a farmer among generations of farmers who have worked this land as far back as records go. His farm in Kilkenny is divided between rearing beef cattle and cultivation for barley. Morgan's also always had an interest in distilling. Could that and his knowledge of barley production be brought together in a way that would create a new opportunity for the farm? Of course they could.

Once Morgan had secured a spirit-manufacturing license, work could start in earnest. He identified a site—a large, old cowshed he wasn't using anymore, but it was in the wrong place. The solution was obvious: Dismantle it stone by stone and rebuild it in the right spot. See? Resourceful. Morgan adds an interesting footnote to this. A local man who looked after the unmaking and remaking of the cowshed turned out to be the grandson of the original builder.

In a very real sense, that little anecdote represents a core principle of Ballykeefe: Everything about it is local. The grain and the water come from the farm. All the spirit will be distilled here—no third-party

Bravissimo! *The first Italian Barison stills installed in Ireland.*

new-make or sourced whiskey will be needed. The pot ale and spent grain will go back to the land or passed on for local animal feed. The entire distilling circle—sowing the barley, harvesting it, storing it; malting, distilling, maturing, and bottling the spirit—will all take place here. The grain-to-glass mantra is not a goal at Ballykeefe; it's fact.

Sustainability is a prime concern here. There is a heat recovery system, rainwater harvesting, water recycling—all part of a commitment, no, an obligation, to the land: to pass it on in a better state.

At the time of our visit, the distillery was not yet producing whiskey, though it is making and exporting some very impressive gins and vodkas. Since production capacity is limited, every bottle can be individually numbered. As master distiller Jamie Baggott says, "Limited edition is the only edition here."

Where the whiskey-making is concerned, they are taking their time with the setup. "It's practically impossible to retrofit in a distillery," Jamie says. "There's only one way to do it and that's to do it right from the start."

Ballykeefe's own new-make is triple-distilled pot still whiskey. In addition to using their own barley, they are experimenting with rye, which is quite unusual in Irish distilling.

For the master distiller, however, nothing is off-limits. "There are no boundaries in what I will play with," Jamie laughs. (And he certainly has an enviable reputation for experimentation, especially with gins.)

For a self-described family farm with an artisan distillery, this is no small undertaking. The equipment is first-rate and the investment has clearly been substantial. The stills are by renowned Italian specialists Barison, and are their first installed in Ireland, as a showcase for their expertise and workmanship.

Visitor tours take you through each stage of the brewing and distilling process, from milling all the way to the warehouse and bottling plant. The tasting room—a reclaimed stable block—has been styled as a comfortable and welcoming Irish country lounge, with an impressive oak bar counter.

Kilkenny was the medieval capital of Ireland. It also claims to be the place where *uisce beatha* was first distilled. Certainly the name appears in the earliest extant written records, which are dated to 1324, and a text known as the *Red Book of Ossory*. There was a long history of distilling in the area that faded away, as was the case with most regional spirit-making. Ballykeefe is the first new distillery here in over two hundred years. Ecologically sound, sustainable, and quality-focused, it marks a welcome return.

Ballykeefe founder Morgan Ging, center.

AT A GLANCE

FIRST DISTILLATION
2017

STILLS
3 Pot Stills (Each: 1,800L)

LPA
Less than 100,000

WHISKEY STYLES
Single Malt & Pot Still

VISITOR CENTER/TOURS
Yes

KEY BOTTLINGS

BALLYKEEFE IRISH WHISKEY

LEINSTER'S GREAT IRISH PUBS

Open sesame—but mind your step.

BERMINGHAM'S

7 Ludlow Street
Navan
County Meath

THE PROVINCE OF
LEINSTER

THE LETTERING ON THE IMMACULATELY
PAINTED FACADE MAY READ "P. BERMINGHAM,"
BUT MOST PEOPLE AROUND HERE STILL CALL
IT "MARMION'S," AFTER MICHAEL MARMION,
THE HUGELY POPULAR AND CHARISMATIC
LATE OWNER.

This is the oldest pub in Navan. It's also tiny. Seriously tiny. With just twenty people in, it's packed. Even so, Michael Marmion always made sure there was room by the fire for musicians.

It's the kind of pub made for conviviality and *craic*, rather than solitary reflection. As Lorraine, Michael's partner says, "People talk to each other in here—there's always a great atmosphere."

The pub has been in the same family since 1884, when it was bought by a young Patrick Bermingham and his sister Jane. Back then it was a standard Irish spirit grocer—food and dry goods counter on one side, pub on the other. Patrick died suddenly, not long after buying the pub, and Jane continued to run the place on her own for the next sixty

years. She never married but did adopt a five-year-old cousin, John Marmion. He inherited the bar in 1948 and in due course passed it on to his son, the aforementioned Michael.

The building hasn't changed much at all since Michael took it over. Even when he gave up the grocery side—which was only in the 1980s—he reused the old counter and shelving. So practically everything you see here is original. There are some quirks around the place, like the copper-colored ventilation system snaking across the ceiling, the collection of ceramic whiskey jars, and the weathervane topped by a leaping horse. Then there are the elaborate wrought-iron roses garlanding the opening to the snug.

When Michael died, his wake was held, naturally, in his pub. On the day of the funeral, the town came to a standstill. People gathered outside Bermingham's and sang many of the songs he loved—a measure

Have a seat. With any luck, this is going to take some time.

of the affection in which he was held, and of the importance of the pub itself to its many regulars.

There's no TV here, no food, no Wi-Fi; but there is live music four nights a week. There's also a very impressive whiskey selection—including some rarities—and an equally impressive range of gins and rums. You'll of course get a fine pint here, and you know what that means. You'll soon be wanting another.

J. O'CONNELL'S

The Green
Skryne
County Meath

THE HILL OF SKRYNE FACES THE HILL
OF TARA, HOME OF THE ANCIENT HIGH
KINGS OF LEGEND. SO THIS IS ANCIENT,
MYTHICAL IRELAND YOU'RE IN. IT'S
THEREFORE TO BE EXPECTED THAT TIME
SEEMS TO RUN A LITTLE DIFFERENTLY.

60

H owever, there is a schedule:
The cows pass by, twice a day, as
they always have. And at four o'clock,
O'Connell's opens its doors.

When the teetotal Mary O'Connell
first came here with her new
husband, James, in the 1940s,
the business they took over was
a thriving spirit grocer, selling
everything from animal feed and
bicycle tires to sausages and jam—as
well as whiskey and bottles of stout.
There are still traces of the grocery
side around the place, but the pub's
the main thing. It's quintessentially
local. Step in and you'll overhear
earnest discussions about cattle
prices and land and always, always
GAA—last weekend's results and
next weekend's fixtures. Around the
walls are newspaper clippings of
sporting success, postcards from the
homesick, photographs of horses, a
copy of Rudyard Kipling's "If," and
community notices. You'll see an
open fire, a long bench facing the bar,
and a creamy paneled ceiling. In the

back room, which has something of the air
of an old-fashioned tea shop, there's a piano.
That's the entertainment center. There's no
food, TV, or radio, let alone Wi-Fi. As far as
the drinks go, the offering is simple, classic:
Guinness and a couple of draft beers; a
handful of whiskeys, gins, and other spirits.
That's about it. Anything else would be
superfluous to the character of the place.

O'Connell's—widely known as "Mrs. O's"
after the woman who continued to run
the pub until she was in her nineties—has
been here since around 1870. It may in
fact be longer; no one's really sure or,
frankly, that concerned. It's been featured
in many movies and commercials and photo
shoots because it's so utterly authentic and
atmospheric. There's nothing pampered
about O'Connell's. It is worn and warm;
functional and plain; a little bit rickety
here and there; and quietly, timelessly
magnificent.

So if you ever find yourself in the realm of
the High Kings, pay your respects to Irish
hospitality here at the shrine of Skryne.

Earnest discussions about cattle prices and land . . .

Rush hour in Skryne. Best just to wait it out in Mrs O's.

SEAN'S BAR

13 Main Street
Athlone
County Westmeath

www.seansbar.ie

HERE'S A THOUGHT. RIGHT AT THE VERY
CENTER OF IRELAND IS THE TOWN OF
ATHLONE. THE TOWN GREW OUT OF A
SETTLEMENT, WHICH GREW UP AROUND
AN OLD INN. SO YOU COULD SAY THAT
AT THE VERY HEART OF IRELAND IS A
PUB—THIS PUB.

THE PROVINCE OF
LEINSTER

It's been here, trading continually, since A.D. 900. That makes Sean's Bar officially the oldest in Ireland, and possibly the world.

The original inn was created at the ford of the mighty River Shannon by a man called Luain, who helped people cross and, presumably, also provided sustenance for the weary traveler. While doing work on the bar in the 1970s, the owners found that some of the old walls were made of wattle and wicker—ancient interlaced twigs and branches bound together with dried mud. And in those walls they also discovered tokens or coins dating back to the tenth century and the inn's original owner.

Amazingly, the bar holds detailed records of every owner since Luain—and of course the original Sean, a local cattle dealer who bought the

place in the 1950s. (A story that Boy George bought the place in 1987 was in fact an April Fools' joke that's still going around.)

The River Shannon has featured prominently in the life of the bar, with many pictures and memorabilia such as antique fishing rods, oars, and driftwood around the place. It's also the explanation for the bar's sloping floor. Long ago, whenever the river would rise and burst its banks, flooding the bar, they just opened the door and let the waters run out.

Welcome to the pub at the center of the (Irish) universe.

How practical. (The flooding problem's been taken care of, but that's no reason to get rid of a perfectly good, if somewhat sloping floor now, is it?)

Sean's is also the only pub in Ireland where you are allowed to pull your own pint of Guinness—under supervision, of course. Unusually, they also have their own brand of stout and even a Sean's Bar Irish Whiskey. Gin aficionados and Irish Coffee devotees are well catered for here, as well. In regard to food, there is none served in the bar, although a proper restaurant is being built in the back.

There's music every evening and a blazing turf fire in the winter. Boy George doesn't know what he's missing.

E. BUTTERFIELD

Main Street
Ballitore
County Kildare

AT A TIME WHEN WOMEN WEREN'T MUCH WELCOME
IN IRISH PUBS, THE FIRST OF THREE GENERATIONS
FROM THE SAME FAMILY WAS RUNNING THIS ONE.

THE PROVINCE OF
LEINSTER

The "E" in E. Butterfield stands for Elizabeth. Today, her granddaughter Lisa Fennin stands behind the bar in the tiny, one-room pub she grew up in, and which she took over from her mother, Philomena. Philomena worked here every day for nearly fifty years. When she died, Lisa held the wake here, in her mother's pub.

Despite the name over the door, the place has always been known as "The Harp," in reference to the sign above the faded "E. Butterfield" lettering. The symbol is significant, for there is history everywhere here in this little village far off the usual tourist path. Some of it is glorious, some tragic, and all of it vividly remembered and endlessly debated, as much of Ireland's history tends to be.

Like so many traditional rural pubs, this also was once the local shop,

and the old wooden grocery drawers are still in place. The shelves are lined with strange bric-a-brac and memorabilia advertising long-vanished products. The building dates back to 1770 and has been a pub since 1780. The farmyard doors, vast open fireplace, ancient counter, and whitewashed walls look like they've been here since then, as does the almost comically uneven flagstone floor. "You're all right coming in," the locals say, "but you have to watch yourself going out." The seats include former church benches and an assortment of stools and chairs randomly distributed about the room. Somehow, it all makes perfect sense.

Lisa, like her mother and grandmother before her, is very fussy about her pints. So you can expect a good one here—a very good one. The whiskey selection is short on choice and long on tradition—the classic triumvirate of Jameson, Paddy, and Powers. No, they don't do food; and no, there's no Wi-Fi. There is a TV, though it doesn't get a lot of use. "People come in for the chat,"

Now, the floor does have just the teeniest, tiniest irregularity . . .

says Lisa. "I think having the TV on would spoil that, don't you?"

Butterfield's has a large open fire, which is lit almost every day. If it's the first Friday of the month, there'll be a proper *seisiún* happening around the hearth. And even if it isn't the first Friday, well, there still might be one. It's that kind of place. Butterfield's is not really a pub for a swift drink. It's not built for life in the fast lane. So, if you get a chance to visit, be prepared to take your time. You'll get where you're going eventually. In the meantime, just settle in and make yourself comfortable. There now, that's better.

O'BRIEN'S

23 Emily Square
Athy
County Kildare

www.obriensbar.com

STEPHEN O'BRIEN WAS A SICKLY MAN. HIS
DOCTOR COUNSELED FRESH COUNTRY AIR,
SO IN 1880 STEPHEN SOLD HIS TEA SHOP
IN DUBLIN, MOVED TO ATHY, MET A LOCAL
WOMAN, AND BOUGHT A SPIRIT GROCER.

THE PROVINCE OF
LEINSTER

E vidently, as his
granddaughter Judith wryly
observes, "The local air clearly did
him a power of good, as he went on
to father eleven children." And in
addition to founding a dynasty, he
left a fine pub legacy.

O'Brien's is an essential part of the
town. Everybody knows it; everyone
has been in it. That's because,
unusually for pubs that began as
spirit grocers, this one still operates
both parts equally—grocery store
and bar. There's a long, single
counter that runs the length of the
place, intersected by a partition
and doorway into the tiny bar in
the back.

The pub is usually called "Frank's,"
after Judith's father, who ran the
place for decades. It's said that he
was the town's greatest champion
and enthusiast. A onetime mayor
of Athy, he used the shopwindow
of O'Brien's to announce every

Grocery in the front, pub in the back: a very practical arrangement.

event, celebrate sporting success, promote every occasion involving the town. That community spirit still imbues the bar today. It's a meeting place, a focal point, and a talking shop.

There are shelves and shelves of books behind the bar. But they're not for decoration. "They're our pre-Google technology," laughs Judith. "They're consulted all the time by regulars. If there's some burning issue being disputed—say about who won the 1927 intermediate county hurling final—we can settle it quickly." The collection is added to all the time. Whenever anyone local writes a book, which is surprisingly often, a copy is ceremoniously added to the O'Brien's Library of Reference.

The outside of the pub hasn't changed in about 140 years. (Look closely and you can still see the rings once used for tethering horses.) The signage is in Irish, and if you do happen to have *cúpla focal*—a couple of words in the mother tongue—feel free to give them an airing here. (There's a sign in

the shop that reads *Tír gan teanga, tír gan dúchas*—"a country without a language is a country without a birthright," so they do take the matter seriously here.)

Like several of the owners we've featured here, Judith has a strong sense of responsibility toward her bar. Yes, it's her family's legacy, but the pub is also an expression of Irish culture. "The work is hard," she says, "but it's worth doing. It matters." That's a noble sentiment, if ever we heard one.

MORRISSEY'S

Main Street
Knocknamoe, Abbeyleix
County Laois

THE PROVINCE OF
LEINSTER

IN DAYS NOT SO LONG GONE BY, IF YOU
WERE IN ABBEYLEIX AND LOOKING FOR
A GROCER'S SHOP, OR AN AUCTIONEER, A
BAKERY, AN UNDERTAKER, A CARPENTER,
OR TRAVEL AGENT, THERE'S ONLY ONE
PLACE YOU'D HAVE GONE: THIS PLACE.

Back then, a pub was the center not just of social life in a town or village but also of commercial life. Today, in Morrissey's there are glorious traces of all its many pasts displayed here in its present—in cabinets and on every shelf and in every nook. There are old scales and measuring equipment here and there among the drawers and ledgers. There's even a branded delivery boy's bike up on a high shelf. (Thankfully, the old hearse that was kept in the yard along with the stockpile of coffins is long gone.)

Built back in 1775—and a shebeen before that—this pub is composed almost entirely of character, from its uneven stone floor right up to its dark-red ceiling. Things in general are a bit aslant and askew. But what's so good about right angles anyway? Current owner Tom Lennon was besotted the instant he set eyes on the place years ago. He still

is. The previous owner had cared for the pub for over fifty years and not changed a thing. Tom sees no great need to either. "It's as nice a pub as you could have," he says modestly, "so why change it?" It's a fair question. "We have turf burning in the old potbellied stove there—and you can't get more organic and modern than that," he adds with a grin. All the fixtures and fittings are original, as are Tom's strong opinions on pubs. "There's a lot of nonsense talked in a place like this. And that's the way it should be. A place like this is an escape from reality. We sorely need that in the world today."

Admittedly, there is a TV in the pub, but it's only used to screen the odd GAA or rugby match. Which then prompts even more conversation. Morrissey's does serve food—good-quality pub grub—and, as you'd expect, serves a fine pint. The drink selection in general is perfectly adequate, and is just what the clientele want. (So if you're in the mood for a mojito, this isn't your best bet.)

Tom Lennon, a man in love with a pub.

Some people have said of Morrissey's
that it's caught in a time warp. Tom
Lennon doesn't view that as an insult
at all. His pub is actually listed as
an officially preserved and protected
building, both inside and out, which
means that changing anything is
difficult. Very difficult. With a bit of
luck, maybe even impossible.

Note the distinctive long, curved bar.

O'SHEA'S

Main Street
Borris
County Carlow

YOU'VE HEARD THE OLD SAYING "COME FOR THE *CRAIC*. STAY FOR A PINT. LEAVE WITH A LIGHT BULB." NO? WELL, MAYBE THAT'S JUST BECAUSE YOU HAVEN'T BEEN TO O'SHEA'S.

Several of the pubs in this book began as spirit grocers. O'Shea's is one of the very few that has kept the grocery side going, albeit in a reduced fashion. But in a town of really only one street, it's just the practical thing to do.

Michael "Bossman" O'Shea bought the business in 1934 and built it up to a thriving store dealing in, well, everything from wool, coal, and grain to farm supplies. Today his grandson, also Michael, runs it, along with his sister, Olivia, and mother, Carmel. They're mindful of the tradition they've been entrusted with, and strive to maintain those old standards of hospitality.

The counter predates Bossman's purchase. It's probably 120 years old, and the dark wood is polished to a glossy, glassy sheen by generations of happy elbows. In fact, much of the bar remains unchanged. The original bacon slicer is still there. A room was

O'Shea's: ready for life's essentials and, more importantly, its nonessentials.

added in the back at some point. Oh, and new stools arrived a year or ten ago, someone remembers, vaguely. The candy-striped bar front is unusual, but then there's also a single Wellington boot hanging from the ceiling. So who's to say what's usual?

Sometimes there's music, sometimes there isn't. But there's always a fire and a friendly greeting. It's a Guinness pub, of course, which doesn't just mean that they serve it here (all pubs do) but that O'Shea's is known for the exceptional quality of its pint. For many an Irish pub-goer this is the ultimate imprimatur. There are some craft beers on offer, too, along with a decent whiskey selection, and a fair few gins. There are no cocktails ("A G&T is as fancy as we get," says Michael). O'Shea's does offer some basic but good pub grub at lunchtime—sandwiches, soups, etc. But people don't really come here for the food. They come because it's a wonderful, uplifting place to spend an hour or two in good company of an evening. And then maybe pick up a box of nails, some fishing line—oh and, yes, a light bulb—on their way home.

LENEHAN'S

10 Castlecomer Road
Kilkenny
County Kilkenny

IN LENEHAN'S YOU'LL HEAR PEOPLE
TALKING ABOUT "THE CATS" AT ALL
HOURS. FOR THE UNINFORMED, THIS
ISN'T SOME LOCAL FELINE OBSESSION.
IT'S A HURLING OBSESSION.

THE PROVINCE OF
LEINSTER

T he mighty county team is nicknamed "The Cats" after an old phrase, "to fight like a Kilkenny cat," meaning to be fierce, tenacious, and determined.

There's lots of Cats memorabilia in here, with the county's black and amber colors hung in bunting above the bar. Of course, there's lots of other stuff, too—old mirrors and advertising signs, ledgers and bills from the bar's former spirit grocer days, ceramic pots, even some old typewriters. You know, the usual bewilderment of curios and ephemera.

Apparently the counter has a slope. They say that when it starts to appear level, it's time to go home. However, most people tend to ignore that advice and stay as long as they possibly can. Because it's lovely in here. Better than that, it's wonderful.

The pub is on a busy corner and is surrounded by the noise and bustle

Welcome to a magical
Kilkenny oasis.

of the modern world. But inside, things are very different. It's timeless, a gem of a traditional rural pub that's somehow been marooned in the city, like a pearl hidden in an oyster.

Predictably, that other great black and amber pairing—Guinness and whiskey— is well respected here. There's also a good selection of gins and some craft beers. Food-wise, there's fresh soup and sandwiches available at lunchtime, and that's about it.

The Lenehans have had this pub since around 1890, but the family has been in the local booze business since the early 1700s. So they know a thing or two about hospitality. They have a gently persistent determination to make you feel comfortable. In that regard, they're a tenacious lot, the Lenehans, a bit like the Cats themselves.

So find yourself a seat, order a drink, and don't worry about the look of that counter. It's perfectly flat. It's the world that's tilted.

A gem of a traditional rural pub that's somehow been marooned in the city . . .

A SHORT HISTORY OF DISTILLING IN DUBLIN

For over a century, Dublin was the center of the whiskey-making world. And at the center of the center was The Liberties—a cluster of narrow streets and alleys that was home to merchants and traders of all kinds. To the poorest of the poor. To a notorious underworld and an even more notorious red-light district in the looming shadow of Christ Church Cathedral.

And of course, it was home to the city's great distilling names, like George Roe & Co., John Jameson and William Jameson, and Power's. In fact, so important were the distillers that the streets became known as the Golden Triangle.

Home to hidden boutiques and more: an alleyway in Temple Bar.

Their businesses prospered and grew. And grew. Their Irish pot still whiskey was prized and celebrated throughout the world. They created a great industry, then saw it disappear through a chain of events (political, technological, and international) that they were largely powerless to influence. And within the space of just over a hundred years, that once-mighty industry was all but gone.

Today, whiskey-making in Dublin is no longer history; it's news. New distilleries such as Dublin Liberties, Diageo's Roe & Co. venture, Pearse Lyons, and Teeling have all set up shop in the former Golden Triangle. Some are already producing whiskey; the rest will be fully operational before 2020.

The lovely Ha'penny Bridge over the equally lovely and alliterative River Liffey.

They are redefining Irish whiskey for new generations of drinkers here in Ireland and around the world, introducing new, lighter styles designed for cocktails—while also mindful of the great tradition of premium pot still *uisce beatha*.

Is the old Golden Triangle seeing a new golden age? Let's just say that the signs are very encouraging. As with all things whiskey, time will tell. And in the meantime, why not just pour yourself a ball of malt and ponder the miracle and mystery and magic of it all.

Sláinte!

Trinity College's Campanile (bell tower)—designed by Charles Lanyon, also the architect of Queen's University in Belfast.

The historic and atmospheric cobbled streets of Temple Bar are—oh look, a pub.

DUBLIN
DISTILLERIES & PUBS

11.

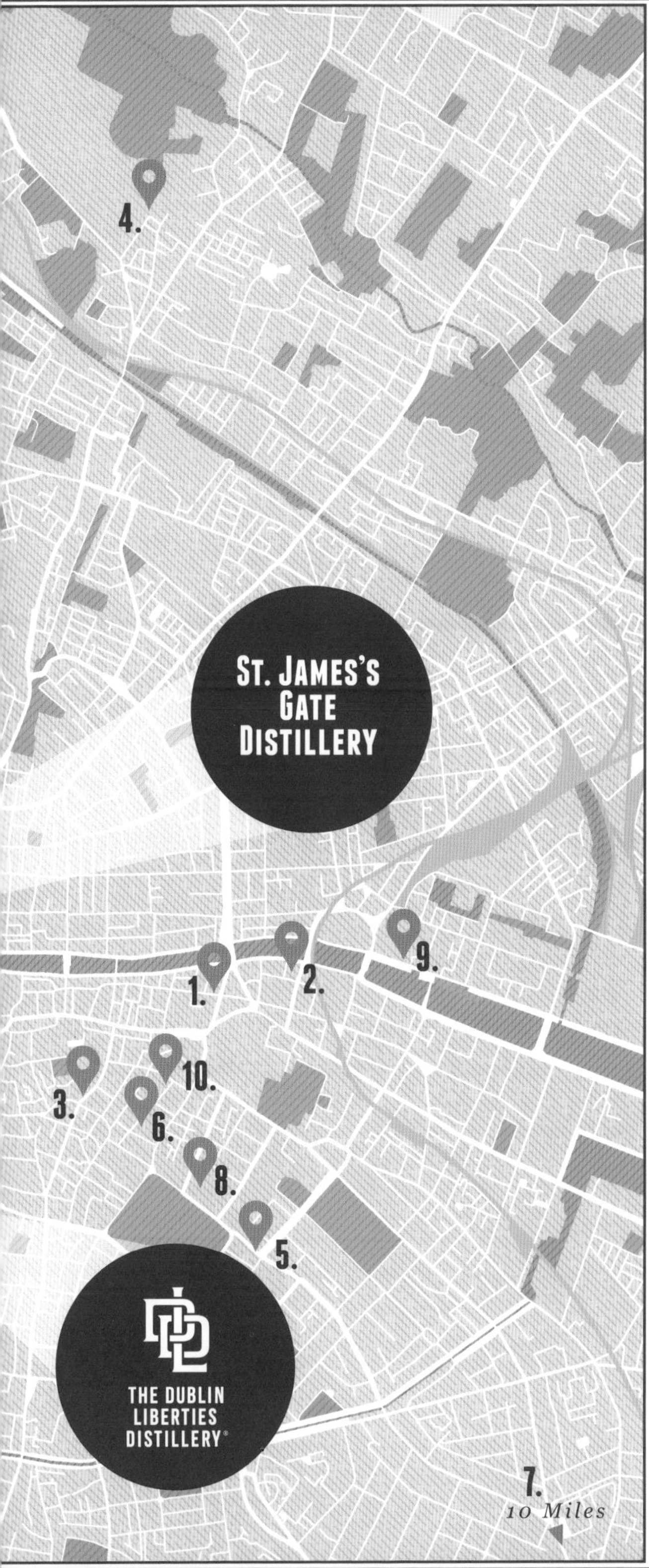

**DUBLIN
DISTILLERIES**
- *Teeling Distillery*
- *The Dublin Liberties Distillery*
- *St. James's Gate Distillery*
- *Pearse Lyons Distillery*

**DUBLIN
PUBS**
1 - *The Palace Bar*
2 - *Mulligan's*
3 - *The Long Hall*
4 - *John Kavanagh's*
5 - *O'Donoghue's*
6 - *McDaid's*
7 - *Johnnie Fox's*

**DUBLIN
WHISKEY STORES**
8 - *Celtic Whiskey Shop & Wines on the Green*
9 - *Mitchell & Son Wine Merchants*
10 - *L. Mulligan Whiskey Shop*
11 - *The Jameson Distillery Bow Street*

St. James's Gate Distillery

THE DUBLIN LIBERTIES DISTILLERY®

10 Miles

DUBLIN
DISTILLERIES
OF TODAY

*It's true: We do treat whiskey-making
with a certain reverence.*

TEELING DISTILLERY

THE PHOENIX IS THE GIVEAWAY. THERE IT IS ON THE LABEL, THE MYTHICAL BIRD ARISING FROM THE BUBBLING POT STILL. AND NOTHING COULD BE MORE APPROPRIATE, FOR HERE INDEED IS THE RESURRECTION OF DUBLIN WHISKEY-MAKING INCARNATE.

13-17 Newmarket
Merchants Quay
Dublin 8

www.teelingdistillery.com

THE CITY OF
DUBLIN

WARRENMOUNT

Another lovely Teeling family portrait.

Teeling is the first new distillery built in the city in 125 years—and, since the closure of John's Lane, the first to operate in over forty years.

But the phoenix doesn't just represent a rebirth of Dublin whiskey-making. It's also the return of an illustrious name to the city. The original Teeling Whiskey Distillery was established by Walter Teeling back in 1782, on Marrowbone Street in The Liberties. The business prospered for nearly a century among many in the so-called Golden Triangle, until it was eventually acquired by William Jameson (a relative of the more famous John). And with that, the name disappeared.

Then in 1989 John Teeling, a distant relative of Walter, opened the Cooley Distillery in County Louth. It was an almost instant success, reviving all-but-forgotten Irish brands such as Tyrconnell and moving production of Kilbeggan to the site.

Beam International (now Beam Suntory) acquired the distillery in 2011. As part of the sale, the family negotiated sixteen thousand casks of mature stock. And with this, the Teeling Whiskey brand itself was launched in 2012.

Having established the name, and with a thriving business as an independent bottler, the next obvious step for the family was a distillery. Which brings us full circle to 2015, to The Liberties and to three gleaming custom-made copper pot stills—named after managing director Jack Teeling's daughters, Alison, Natalie, and Rebecca. The master distiller is Alex Chasko, who was previously innovations manager at Cooley.

Be original, a maverick, an innovator: This is the key to the Teeling approach and, as they see it, both the opportunity and challenge for the independent distiller. They have great respect for the big-name Irish distillers but aren't trying to replicate what they do. Brothers Jack and Stephen Teeling want their whiskey to find its own space in the market. So they have opted for handcrafted, small-batch bottlings of superior quality. And already the awards are coming, including Best Irish Single Malt and Best Irish Single Grain. Crucial to that endeavor is Alex Chasko—a sort of maverick's maverick who first became known at Kilbeggan for his imaginative work on cask finishes with bog oak, and using rye in mashbills.

He has now installed his laboratory at Teeling, and is pursuing even greater heights of creativity and originality. But—and this is a big but—Team Teeling is not interested in innovation for its own sake. They see great, untapped potential for Irish whiskey—and so, they ask, why would we simply stick to the tried and tested? Why seek to reinvent the wheel? Why indeed. Yes, this is a place where they actively experiment with finishing, using various rum, red wine, ex-bourbon, and Calvados casks. (Their single malt is finished in no fewer than five different casks, including sherry, white Burgundy, Madeira, port, and cabernet sauvignon.) Almost everything is double-distilled, though they are also naturally looking at triple-distillation. They are also working to push the boundaries even further, by using pine fermenters, different yeast strains, and experimenting with mashbills (for example, using crystal malt).

The Teelings are at pains to point out that theirs is a working, urban distillery, not a facsimile of one. It's why they call it The Spirit of Dublin. Tours allow you to experience firsthand the sight, sound, and smell of a fully functioning whiskey distillery.

Keeping it in the family: The stills are named after the managing director's daughters.

After the tour you can visit the Bang Bang Bar (named after a notorious Liberties character) for a cocktail or a guided comparative tasting. You can even fill your own bottle of Teeling whiskey to take away.

At Teeling they believe there's room for something genuinely different, something for people perhaps new to Irish whiskey to discover. And that's what they're trying to create. When the family revived the name and opened the distillery, they were mindful of their own place in the city's industrial history but had a new vision: to connect with a new generation.

There's a confident, creative air about Teeling, from the innovative cask maturation techniques to the willingness to explore unusual blends and grain combinations. It's an idea that's finding a warm and eager reception here in Ireland, but also throughout the world, with over fifty countries clamoring for these genuinely different whiskeys. A recent investment and minority stake by Bacardi has secured U.S. distribution for Teeling into the largest market for Irish whiskey—and is therefore likely to take the brand to even greater heights over the next few years.

AT A GLANCE

FIRST DISTILLATION
2015

STILLS
3 Pot Stills (Alison 15,000L, Natalie 10,000L, Rebecca 9,000L)

LPA
500,000

WHISKEY STYLES
Single Malt & Pot Still

VISITOR CENTER/TOURS
Yes

KEY BOTTLINGS

TEELING SMALL BATCH
ABV: 46%

TEELING SINGLE GRAIN
ABV: 46%

TEELING SINGLE MALT
ABV: 46%

TEELING VINTAGE RESERVE 33 SINGLE MALT
ABV: 42.9%
(Note: This is Ireland's oldest bottled whiskey)

BRABAZON SERIES
Single malts matured in fortified wine casks; Volume 1: sherry and Volume 2: port

THE DUBLIN LIBERTIES DISTILLERY

THE LIBERTIES IS A VERY OLD PART OF THE CITY; QUINTESSENTIAL DUBLIN, SOME SAY. IT GREW UP BEYOND THE ANCIENT CITY WALLS AND SOVEREIGN RULE, INDEPENDENT, HARDWORKING, AND PLAINSPOKEN— BUT ALWAYS WELCOMING.

33 Mill Street
Merchants Quay
Dublin 8

www.thedublinlibertiesdistillery.com

There was a long and glorious tradition of distilling centered in the area's maze of narrow streets. However, by the early part of the twentieth century the industry had all but dwindled away. Now it's back, and in a big way.

Owner Quintessential Brands Group has invested over €15 million (approximately $17 million) in a new craft whiskey distillery with, crucially, its own natural spring water source. There are also plans for a state-of-the-art visitor center that expects to receive around seventy-five thousand visitors a year.

The Dublin Liberties building itself is a twenty-five thousand square foot space with a history dating back over three hundred years. During that time it has been everything from a flour mill to a lumberyard and a tannery. The historic frontage of the building and many original features have been retained, while the interior showcases the best of today's distilling technology. By blending the historic and the contemporary, the company aims to create a vivid sense of what has come before.

THE CITY OF
DUBLIN

WARRENMOUNT

Bringing it all back home: Whiskey-making returns to The Liberties.

Is it a bird? Is it a plane? Better: It's a fermenter.

Though the stock is currently sourced from Cooley, once completed, the operation will include a full malt distillery capable of double and triple distillation. It will be home to the Dubliner and the Dublin Liberties ranges, as well as Dead Rabbit Irish Whiskey—all overseen by Darryl McNally, one of the most distinguished master distillers working in Ireland today. Darryl spent almost twenty years at Bushmills up on the north Antrim coast, before The Liberties came calling.

Darryl McNally, master distiller and distillery manager.

"Our goal is to become one of the leading whiskey producers in Ireland," he said. "We're building a world-class distillery in the heart of Dublin with a visitor experience like no other. It will perfectly complement the other developments in what is fast becoming the most exciting part of Dublin." Dubliner comprises two blends—a light, easy-drinking three-year-old and a more complex five-year-old matured in bourbon casks. There is also a whiskey and honeycomb liqueur, as well as a ten-year-old single malt.

There are two bottlings in the Dublin Liberties range: Oak Devil, a bourbon-cask-aged blend of premium malt and grain whiskeys; and Copper Alley, a single malt aged for ten years in bourbon casks and finished in sherry butts. These two whiskeys are named after intriguing elements drawn from the colorful history of The Liberties—once a wild and wayward quarter of old Dublin that was scorned by high society during the day, and enthusiastically frequented by them at night . . .

"Our goal is to become one of the leading whiskey producers in Ireland..."

AT A GLANCE

FIRST DISTILLATION
2018 (expected)

STILLS
3 Pot Stills (Wash Still 10,000L, Intermediate Still 6,000L, Spirit Still 6,000L)

LPA
700,000 (projected)

STYLES
Single Malt & Pot Still

VISITOR CENTER/TOURS
Yes, when complete

KEY BOTTLINGS

DEAD RABBIT IRISH WHISKEY
ABV: 44%

DUBLIN LIBERTIES IRISH WHISKEY:

COPPER ALLEY 10-YEAR-OLD SINGLE MALT
ABV: 46%

OAK DEVIL BLEND
ABV: 46%

THE DUBLINER RANGE:

DUBLINER BLENDED IRISH WHISKEY
ABV: 40%

DUBLINER 10-YEAR-OLD SINGLE MALT
ABV: 42%

ST. JAMES'S GATE DISTILLERY

ST. JAMES'S GATE IS KNOWN THROUGHOUT THE WORLD AS THE HOME OF GUINNESS. TODAY, THE VAST SITE ALSO HOUSES A DISTILLERY THAT REVIVES AN ILLUSTRIOUS NAME FROM DUBLIN'S WHISKEY-MAKING HISTORY.

St. James's Gate
Dublin 8

THE CITY OF
DUBLIN

ARBOUR HILL

MOUNT BROWN

Back in the 1880s, George Roe's seventeen-acre distillery was the biggest in Ireland, possibly even in the world. It was easily the dominant presence shaping the golden age of Irish whiskey-making, dwarfing the combined production of both Jameson and Powers. A family business, it grew both by amalgamation and acquisition. At its height, the distillery was producing over two million gallons of pot still whiskey a year. Its vast lofts could hold over one hundred thousand barrels of grain, and the conveyor belt stretched for a full mile.

This economic might brought the Roe family vast wealth and influence in Victorian Dublin society. They funded the extension of Christ Church Cathedral, and George himself was lord mayor of the city three times.

In 1891, with the growing challenge from Scottish blended whiskies, the distillery joined forces with the DWD Distillery on Jones Road and the William Jameson Distillery on Marrowbone Lane to form the Dublin Distillers Company.

The home of the black stuff—and now also the amber stuff.

Built in 1757, the 150-foot-tall St. Patrick's Tower is the only remaining landmark from the original George Roe Distillery.

However, all three firms continued to produce pot still whiskey under their own names—and therefore competed with each other, in addition to the Scottish blends. But none of the three Dublin firms enjoyed the reputation of Jameson or Powers.

By the turn of the century, the problems were mounting, compounded by social, political, and economic instabilities in Ireland. Then came Prohibition in the United States. Almost overnight the company's key market vanished. Production dwindled, vast stocks remained unsold, and in 1923 the great distillery closed. Today, all that remains on the site is the landmark St. Patrick's Tower—a former windmill that once helped power some of the distillery's operations—and a solitary ancient pear tree that still flowers and bears fruit.

Now, nearly a century later, the tower and pear tree sit facing the new home of Roe & Co Whiskey. This once-great name is back, housed in the former Guinness power station on Thomas Street—across the road from St. James's Gate and Ireland's leading tourist attraction, the Guinness Storehouse.

George Roe and Guinness, two major names of Dublin's distilling and brewing history, were once somewhat wary, even quarrelsome neighbors. (It was said at the time that the Guinness brewers considered their stout "the nurse of the people" and spirits such as whiskey "the curse of the people.") Now, Guinness owner Diageo has undertaken the task to revive the Roe name in an ambitious venture to explore the possibilities of a resurgent Irish whiskey market, and to breathe new life into The Liberties. There's a lot of Diageo expertise and investment behind the €25 million-plus venture (around $29 million), with its gleaming stills, planned state-of-the-art visitor center, and on-site training facility.

Full-scale production is due to begin in 2019. In contrast with the historical single pot still style of George Roe whiskey, Diageo's will be a three-still, 100 percent single malt operation. This distillery is already producing its first line from meticulously selected stocks. Roe & Co is a blend of premium Irish malt and grain whiskeys, all triple-distilled and aged in ex-bourbon American oak casks. It's very smooth and very accessible, with notes of pear, soft spice, and a hint

Roe & Co: A once-great name is back—and is great again.

of vanilla from the high proportion of first-fill casks used in the blend.

This is a whiskey that took its time to get here. Master blender Caroline Martin created over a hundred versions before finding exactly what she was looking for. (If you're interested, it was number 106.) Along the way, she and Diageo Whiskey Ambassador Peter O'Connor also enlisted the help of a select group of leading Dublin barmen and mixologists to trial various blends and provide feedback. The goal was to create a distinctively Irish whiskey that would work on its own but would especially excel in cocktails—an area that the owners believe is significantly underdeveloped.

In a nod to the illustrious past of its name, the distinctive Roe & Co bottle features the tower—with its distinctive blue copper roof—and, of course, a solitary and still flowering pear tree. Other whiskeys are already in the pipeline (there are even whispers of a single malt). So are we witnessing the birth of a new golden age? A wise man wouldn't bet against it.

AT A GLANCE

FIRST DISTILLATION
2019 (expected)

STILLS
3 Pot Stills (Wash Still 14,000L, Intermediate Still 6,600L, Spirit Still 5,000L)

LPA
500,000

WHISKEY STYLES
Single Malt

VISITOR CENTER
Yes, when complete

KEY BOTTLINGS

ROE & CO BLENDED IRISH WHISKEY
ABV: 45%

DUBLIN DISTILLERIES OF TODAY

PEARSE LYONS DISTILLERY

IT TAKES A LOT OF WORK TO CREATE A MODERN DISTILLERY. IT TAKES EVEN MORE WITH A BUILDING LIKE THIS ONE, THE HISTORIC AND LONG-DECONSECRATED CHURCH OF ST. JAMES IN THE LIBERTIES.

121-122 James Street
Dublin 8

www.pearselyonsdistillery.com

THE CITY OF
DUBLIN

ARBOUR HILL

MOUNT BROWN

I t is an officially listed (i.e., protected) building, where some of the walls are three feet thick, where there were single wooden rafters thirty feet long, and where there were also mighty expanses of disintegrating concrete and rusting iron to be removed.

And that's not all. Next to the church is the ancient graveyard, which has seen centuries of burials, including Mark Rainsford (1709), whose brewery would eventually be bought by one Arthur Guinness. James Power, founder of the whiskey dynasty, was also laid to rest here. To lift as much as a stone in this graveyard has meant archaeological licenses, complex planning agreements, cataloging, and even exhumation permits. All of this has vastly contributed to the time and costs entailed in establishing a distillery on this spot.

Yet here it is. And what a place—with its acreages of gleaming burnished copper, its magnificent glass spire, its stained-glass depictions of the distilling story spilling a kaleidoscope of colors across the floors and walls. In a sense, this is a

The stained-glass windows tell the venerable story of distillation.

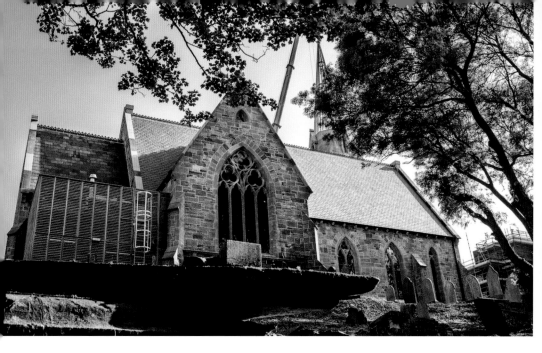

brand-new distillery that's been eight hundred years in the making. The church dates back to the late twelfth century: before Magna Carta, the discovery of America, Chaucer, and Shakespeare; before the Renaissance, the French Revolution, the Industrial Revolution, and the Great War. Even before whiskey.

For the last half-century, the building lay derelict. In the decades before it had been used and misused by various merchants and traders (hence the concrete), until it was finally abandoned altogether. Then the late Dr. Pearse Lyons, founder and president of the Kentucky-based global Alltech group, born in Dundalk and educated in Dublin, rediscovered it. He discovered something else, too: that his grandfather was buried in the graveyard, along with eight other distant relatives. And there were other connections: Dr. Pearse's mother came from a family of coopers in The Liberties. The restoration of the church quickly became a true passion project that also paid tribute to the area's unique distilling history.

Dr. Lyons had once been a brewer himself (at Guinness) and a distiller (at Midleton). Then, armed with a master's degree in brewing science and a PhD in biochemistry, he left Ireland for the United States. In Kentucky, he put his highly specialized knowledge of yeasts to use in a different field—namely animal nutrition. He founded Alltech—today a global group with interests in animal feeds, as well as brewing and distilling. Having returned to Ireland, he also returned to his old dream of a distillery. The meticulous structural and restoration work on the church took about four years. It included the installation of the stunning glass spire—known locally as the

Liberties Lantern. And then there are those stained-glass windows. Of the four, three illustrate the story of whiskey-making. The fourth depicts the Camino de Santiago de Compostela pilgrimage of St. James, for whom the church was originally consecrated.

The centerpieces of the distillery itself are quite unique: an all-copper brewing system and two copper stills from Kentucky that produced the first single malt, "a new Irish whiskey with a Kentucky flair." The wash still, "Mighty Mollie," has an unusual design with a ball and neck arrangement designed to reflux during distillation, resulting in a lighter style of spirit. The spirit still, "Little Lizzie," features four rectification plates in its neck to help remove volatile alcohols during production. (This arrangement is unusual in Irish distilling, though is more common in the United States, where the stills were made.)

Ambitions for the Dublin distillery are modest in terms of volume, and will focus on two double-distilled single malts aged in former bourbon casks. The first is described as a sipping whiskey that mixes well—a sort of superior entry-level whiskey. The second will be aged in Kentucky ale barrels and finished in sherry and bourbon casks. The company had its stills installed off-site in County Carlow for a number of years, building up stock until the building was ready. Now the work is finished and the former church—mirabile dictu—is once again concentrating on matters of the spirit, one drop at a time.

The devotion to distillation is illuminating.

AT A GLANCE

FIRST DISTILLATION
2017

STILLS
"Mighty Mollie," 2,400L,
"Little Lizzie," 1,200L

LPA
75,000

STYLES
Single Malt, Pot Still & Grain

VISITOR CENTER/TOURS
Yes

KEY BOTTLINGS

PEARSE LYONS THE ORIGINAL BLEND
ABV: 42%

**PEARSE LYONS DISTILLER'S CHOICE
BLENDED IRISH WHISKEY**
ABV: 42%

PEARSE LYONS COOPER'S SELECT
ABV: 42%

**PEARSE LYONS FOUNDER'S CHOICE
12-YEAR-OLD SINGLE MALT**
ABV: 42%

DUBLIN'S GREAT IRISH PUBS

*Mind your heads—urgent pint
coming through.*

THE PALACE BAR

21 Fleet Street
Dublin 2
www.thepalacebardublin.com

THE CITY OF
DUBLIN

O'CONNELL ST

TRINITY

BUILT IN 1823—AND LARGELY UNTOUCHED
SINCE THE 1880s—THE PALACE BAR IS ONE
OF THE CITY'S OLDEST PUBS, PERHAPS ITS
BEST-PRESERVED EXAMPLE OF VICTORIAN
ARCHITECTURE, AND ALMOST CERTAINLY
ITS WORDIEST ONE.

Up until the 1950s the offices of both the *Irish Times* and *Irish Press* were located just across the street. This made the Palace the watering hole of choice for hard-drinking journalists. In fact, the back room came to be known as the "Intensive Care Unit" due to the number of "cures" dispensed there. Others knew it as the "Alligator Pit," where the unwary risked decapitation by sheer biting force of whiskey-fueled wit.

Writers, too, flocked to the Palace. Samuel Beckett, Brendan Behan, Patrick Kavanagh, and John B. Keane were all regulars at one time, and their portraits appear everywhere here. But the writer most closely associated with the Palace is the triple-named Brian O'Nolan a.k.a. Flann O'Brien a.k.a. Myles na gCopaleen, who, it was said, drank for all three. The author of the comic masterpiece *At-Swim-Two-Birds* even brought his own jigger to double-check the bartender's pour. That's dedication.

Take your seat in the temple of talk.

O'Nolan—or Myles—died on the first of April 1966. Ever since, the Palace has hosted its "Myles's Day" on that comedically apposite date. The bar also has a passage from *At-Swim* etched on its window.

The Palace has been owned by the Aherne family since 1946, when it was acquired by the grandfather of current manager Willie Aherne. Three generations of his family lived on the floor above the pub until it was turned into another bar. Now known as the Whiskey Palace, this is an intimate space with a vast collection of miniature Powers whiskey bottles suspended from the ceiling. Also on display is the full collection of Midleton Irish whiskey vintages, which Willie fondly calls "my retirement fund."

label range in 2012: a nine-year-old single cask, a twelve-year-old single malt, a fourteen-year-old single malt, and a limited edition single malt.

"A bird is known by its song, a man by his conversation"

Willie Aherne

Unusually, the Palace also has its own house whiskey. In conjunction with Cooley Distillery, Willie revived the Palace's own

The main bar is free of background music—as Willie says, "it detracts from the music of conversation." Upstairs, the Whiskey Palace offers quiet jazz and blues played on vinyl. Thursday nights feature an Irish traditional music *seisiún*.

If you get a chance to visit, take it. And be sure to take plenty of time with you, too.

MULLIGAN'S

8 Poolbeg Street
Dublin 2
www.mulligans.ie

THE CITY OF
DUBLIN

O'CONNELL ST

TRINITY

IT WAS A STRANGE REQUEST—NO QUESTION ABOUT IT—BUT THEY OBLIGED NONETHELESS. AND THAT IS WHY DEEP WITHIN THE DARK RECESSES OF THE BIG GRANDFATHER CLOCK IN MULLIGAN'S ARE INTERRED THE ASHES OF THE LATE BILLY BROOKS CARR OF HOUSTON, TEXAS. HE WAS A MAN WITH A GREAT AND ABIDING LOVE FOR THIS PUB. AND NOW HE'S HERE ALL THE TIME.

This is just one of a thousand anecdotes about the grand old pub of Poolbeg Street. James Joyce mentions it in *Dubliners* (if you're interested, it's in "Counterparts"). Judy Garland drank here when she was working at the nearby Theatre Royal. JFK sank a few pints when he was a thirsty young journalist-about-town. Many of Ireland's best-known scribblers found both mischief and copy here. Poets, singers, students, revolutionaries, civil servants, locals: Everyone who has ever gone drinking in Dublin has probably been here at some time. And of course, Mulligan's also boasts the twin imprimatur of all the city's great pubs: firstly, ghosts; and secondly, Brendan Behan (drank here; barred here).

What makes Mulligan's so special? Ah well, now. Gary Cusack, the current owner, who runs it along with his brother Ger, has a theory. "Keep it simple. A great pint. Staff with a bit of banter about them. Look after everybody and treat everybody the same. If you do all that, you've done a lot."

The building itself has quite a part to play, as well, of course. From its smart black and red exterior to its warm, surprisingly bright and comfortable interior, the place has said "Welcome All" for over two hundred years.

The Cusack boys took over the pub from their father, Tommy, who spent fifty-five years here. And indeed, long tenures are a factor at Mulligan's. Many of the staff have worked for decades in the place, and Gary himself has been here around thirty years. During that time he's known entire generations of customers. Although the city has been greatly transformed since Tommy's day, Gary sees no need for much change in the pub. So, no cocktails. No Irish Coffee ("I say I don't have the cream"). No food, no music: just atmosphere. And that's more than enough for the regulars and visitors alike. There is a TV, but it's off much more than it's on—and even then, mostly for sport (GAA or rugby).

Is the Guinness the best you'll find in the city? "Well, it's up there," concedes Gary modestly, "because we look after it." And they do, practically tiptoeing around the newly delivered kegs in the cellar, as they settle themselves after the indignity of transportation. The whiskey offering—which currently stands at around fifteen—features the classics (Powers, Jameson, and Bushmills), as well as a number of interesting newer names. There's also around a dozen gins.

It's been said that all art aspires to the condition of music. If so, then perhaps all pubs aspire to the condition of Mulligan's, a harmonious phenomenon that seems to improve with every customer, every yarn, and every jar.

This is what over two hundred years of craic, *jars, and conviviality gets you. Perfection.*

THE LONG HALL

51 South Great George's Street
Dublin 2

THERE ARE TWO CLOCKS IN THE LONG HALL.
THE OLD ONE WAS INSTALLED IN 1881; THE
NEW ONE, JUST RECENTLY, IN 1911. THEY'RE
STILL GETTING USED TO THE NEW ONE.
THAT'S THE KIND OF PLACE THIS IS. IT'S
UNDERSTANDABLE: THERE'S BEEN A HOSTELRY
ON THIS SPOT SINCE 1766. AND ALL THAT
HISTORY DOES LEND A CERTAIN PERSPECTIVE.

There's time—and there's Long Hall time . . .

Time stands still here, which is part of what makes The Long Hall special. Well, just look around you. Take in that warm, jeweled light; that dark polished wood; the soft, low hum of conversation. You couldn't rush yourself here if you tried. So no one does.

The Long Hall is probably the best intact example of a Victorian-era pub not just in Dublin but in Ireland. Apart from some new wiring and some mirrors added yesterday (well, fifty years ago), not much else has changed since the nineteenth century. In any case, the pub is listed on the historic-buildings register, so making alterations now would be difficult, even if anyone wanted to (which, frankly, they don't).

This is a bar that welcomes everyone—from visiting superstars to the regulars—and treats them all the same. No status or special

cosseted—carefully handled, stored, chilled, and rotated to ensure their prized consistency. Each week every single glass is washed by hand using a special detergent. Then on a daily basis they are machine washed using only hot water, and air-dried. And when drinking Guinness, the glass matters a lot. At The Long Hall, it's strictly the classic "tulip" version, or "the pagan glass," as one customer dubbed it.

What about the whiskey? At present you'll find over sixty bottles, "and if we had the space we could have 160!" says Marcus. For the pub's 250th anniversary, they commissioned a single-cask whiskey from Powers (fourteen-year-old, ex-bourbon barrel). Ask nicely and you might set eyes on a bottle.

treatment is given because the place itself is special enough. It's always the star.

"The key," says current owner Marcus Houlihan, "is to treat people as if they were in your own house. We go out of our way to make them feel comfortable." Marcus isn't really convinced by the term "owner," stating, "You don't really own a gem like this. You're just the custodian—and you have to leave it better than you found it."

Many of the staff have been here for a very long time—over forty years in the case of the bar manager. That continuity brings with it a fierce loyalty and respect verging on reverence. Some regulars who have long since moved away from the area continue to travel from as far away as fifty miles to this, their "local."

And what are they traveling for? The ambience, of course; the familiarity, the hospitality, and the Guinness. As is the case with all our Great Irish Pubs, The Long Hall's is one pampered pint. The kegs are

The Long Hall doesn't do food—not even the seemingly ubiquitous Dublin toasted sandwich. There's no need: The pub is surrounded by restaurants. Marcus lets them handle what they're best at, and The Long Hall does the same.

DUBLIN'S GREAT IRISH PUBS

JOHN KAVANAGH'S
a.k.a. The Gravedigger's

1 Prospect Square
Glasnevin
Dublin 9

BRENDAN BEHAN—RIOTOUSLY ROISTERING
WRITER, POET, PLAYWRIGHT, AND DRINKER—
IS BURIED AT GLASNEVIN CEMETERY IN
DUBLIN. IT'S EASY TO SPOT HIS GRAVE: IT
OFTEN HAS A PINT OF GUINNESS PLACED ON
TOP. AND THAT PINT COMES FROM NEXT DOOR,
FROM KAVANAGH'S, MORE COMMONLY KNOWN
AS THE GRAVEDIGGER'S. WELL, BRENDAN
ALWAYS WAS VERY FUSSY.

The road into the city from the airport will take you past here; and indeed, many travelers do come directly here, luggage in tow. Step inside and you'll see why. It's incredibly beautiful—all aged dark wood and soft low light—which is doubtless why it has been featured in many movies and commercials. If you want to see the quintessential traditional Irish pub, then look no further.

Seven generations of Kavanaghs have stood behind this bar, all the way back to 1833. For many years this was a rough-and-tumble pub that required a firm hand, such as that of the redoubtable Josie Kavanagh, whose imperious reign spanned two world wars and the War of Independence at home. Of course, it's an eminently civilized spot now, with a sophisticated food offering that includes a hearty tapas menu.

In other respects, The Gravedigger's is still resolutely no-nonsense. There's no music here, and no TV. A slice of lemon in a G&T is as exotic as you'll get. Don't even bother asking for a cocktail—but then again, why would you? In regard to the quality of the Guinness here, Ciaran Kavanagh—who runs the kitchen while his sister Anne takes care of the pub—modestly says, "You might get as good elsewhere, but you'll not get better."

We'd go further. We think they have the best pint in Dublin. Which thus makes it the best in Ireland and therefore this world (and—if you're listening, Brendan—the next). Add that to a fine whiskey and gin selections, and you've got something very special indeed.

Ciaran and Anne grew up here, in an apartment above the bar. He remembers the relevance of this on a particularly significant day in the city's history—the funeral of Luke Kelly of The Dubliners.

The choice of generations—and fussy late playwrights.

All of Ireland's music leading lights were there: traditional, folk, and rock. As Ciaran recalls, "they came to the pub and started tuning up. My father put a stop to it straight away. He said, 'Listen, I have people in here every night trying to sing. I don't let them. My kids are upstairs, they can't sleep, and my wife is unhappy. So no singing, no matter who you are. Take it outside!'" And so they did and went over to the green across the way with their drinks. It turned into an all-day free concert by superstars.

Kavanagh's also claims to be the origin of the term "jar" for a pint. The gravediggers in Glasnevin preferred to drink outside but weren't allowed to take glasses from the pub. So they began to bring their own containers—such as earthenware pots and jars. Like all such stories, it may be true, it may not be (and naturally there are competing versions); but it's all still good for the telling, and that's what matters. Perhaps predictably, given the location, Kavanagh's also has a couple of resident ghosts, including a mysterious lady who's been seen crossing the room, and an old regular called Chalky. By all accounts, they don't bother anyone; they just miss the *craic*, which is completely understandable.

O'DONOGHUE'S

15 Merrion Row
Dublin 2

www.odonoghues.ie

THE CITY OF
DUBLIN

TRINITY

St STEPHEN'S
GREEN

SOME OF THE GREAT IRISH BARS,
ESPECIALLY IN DUBLIN, ARE THE PRODUCT
OF METICULOUS VICTORIAN PLANNING
FOLLOWED BY LONG DECADES OF SCRUPULOUS
STEWARDSHIP. AND THEN THERE ARE PUBS
LIKE O'DONOGHUE'S. (CORRECTION: THERE
ARE NO PUBS LIKE O'DONOGHUE'S.)

O'DONOGHUE'S

This place doesn't feel as though it was designed or planned. It feels as though it simply surfaced on Merrion Row of its own volition. There may not be a straight line or a right angle or even a level floor in the place. The Victorians would be aghast. The rest of us are just having too good a time.

The pub has been in family hands for nearly a century but gained its current name in 1934, when Paddy and Maureen O'Donoghue took over. Today, the custodians are the Barden family—Kevin, his sister, Carol, his uncle, Declan, and his father, Oliver ("still the boss").

Music's the thing in O'Donoghue's—real, proper Irish music, seven nights a week, and all day Sunday, including out in the beer garden. There are no amps, no mics, no formal groups. Just people in a corner going for it—or as they say in Dublin, "giving it a lash." Famously,

The Dubliners formed here back in the early sixties, and there are portraits of the beardy lads all over the walls, along with the likes of The Fureys, Seamus Ennis, and Joe Heaney. The national treasure that is Christy Moore played here many times, as has more or less the entire who's who of Irish music, and then some. The pub itself has even been celebrated in song, as well, most notably by Andy Irvine, whose *O'Donoghue's* paints an affectionate portrait of the pub in the sixties. It's hard to see how everyone fits in—this isn't a big place—but where there's a will . . .

Like many pubs of this vintage, the upstairs was once the living quarters of the publican's family. In O'Donoghue's those quarters have since been converted into guest rooms that can be booked. As Kevin puts it, "not B&B, just the B." Which leads us to another consideration: food. Choice is, let's say, limited. Rolls or crisps—take your pick.

But when it comes to whiskey, there's much greater variety on offer, with around thirty

Here it's always been about the singer and the song.

The Dubliners formed here back in the early sixties . . .

brands currently jostling for space. Gin, too, has become much more popular of late, and the bar carries an impressive range of established as well as boutique and craft brands. Understandably, O'Donoghue's is almost always busy. You might think that would cause a problem getting served a Guinness, given that it takes nearly two minutes to pour a pint. Never fear: They've got a system. There's a barman focused solely on just working the tap, lining up rows of creamy pints on the bar, then making his way back along the rows, topping them off. And then they use their secret weapon: a step arrangement built behind the bar that allows the other barman to deliver your pint over the heads of the thirsty throng. It's quite a sight.

McDAID'S

3 Harry Street
Dublin 2

www.mcdaidspub.com

THE CITY OF
DUBLIN

TRINITY

ST STEPHEN'S
GREEN

AFTER MORE THAN TWENTY YEARS, OLIVER COSGRAVE STILL CAN'T BELIEVE HIS LUCK. "I LOVE THIS PUB," HE SAYS. "I IDOLIZE IT." A SHREWD AND EXPERIENCED BUSINESSMAN, HE KNEW HE WAS GETTING SOMETHING SPECIAL WHEN HE BOUGHT McDAID'S. HE JUST DIDN'T KNOW HOW SPECIAL.

McDAID'S

Outside, there's not much to get excited about. There are fancier, olde-worldier, cooler-looking pubs everywhere. Ah, but with McDaid's, all the magic is inside.

There's been a hostelry of sorts on this spot since 1799. At one time, there was also, bizarrely, a morgue. "And there's all sorts of shenanigans and stories about that," Oliver adds, mysteriously. The fame of the pub in its current, sublime Victorian incarnation owes more to its association with writers like Patrick Kavanagh, Brian O'Nolan/Flann O'Brien, Austin Clarke, Anthony Cronin, J.P. Donleavy, Liam O'Flaherty, and, of course, Brendan Behan—who seems to be "most strongly associated with" practically every Dublin boozer you enter. There are portraits of these and other greats throughout the bar.

These days, the pub is famous enough to attract celebrities, visiting dignitaries, tourists of course, but also locals—the regulars whose pints are graciously placed in front of them as soon as they take their seats in their usual spots. That's the kind of place this is.

The interior is exquisite—warm, dark wood; leather-topped stools and red benches; hand-painted mosaic tiles; gleaming brass. There are both nooks and crannies aplenty here, each one cradling some curio from days gone by. Above the bar is an old steamer trunk, home at last.

Behind the bar itself is a particularly fine array of Irish whiskeys, including some real rarities. The Guinness is, of course, outstanding, and there is also a goodly selection of beers and ales. There's no food offering to speak of, so let's not.

Situated in a quiet corner just off bustling Grafton Street, McDaid's is an oasis of

Modest on the outside, magic on the inside.

civility and relaxed, easy charm. The pub is very small, and it does get busy. There is a quieter upstairs bar, if you're prepared to brave the dizzying ascent up the narrow staircase.

There's nothing contrived about this pub. It's traditional, old-fashioned; you might even say quaint. But if you want to experience the real thing, the authentic, quintessential Irish pub, well here's your man.

At one time, there was also, bizarrely, a morgue . . .

JOHNNIE FOX'S

Glencullen
County Dublin
www.jfp.ie

THE COUNTY OF
DUBLIN

EATH

DUBLIN

KILDARE

DUBLIN
CITY

WICKLOW

YOU KNOW WHERE YOU ARE WITH A PUB THAT OFFERS "A HOOLEY AND SHENANIGANS EVERY NIGHT." A PUB THAT SAYS, "WE'VE SPENT OVER 200 YEARS GETTING READY FOR TONIGHT." WHERE A SIGN READS, "THE FOX IS ON THE MOUNTAIN AND THE *CRAIC* IS MIGHTY."

Not so much a pub as an experience.

Y ou know exactly where you are: You're here, about thirty minutes from Dublin city center in lovely Glencullen in the even lovelier Wicklow mountains, and you're about to enter the alternative universe that is Johnnie Fox's, which is Ireland's highest pub. (Supposedly. Purportedly. Not.)

The pub was established in 1798, the year of the Irish Rebellion led by Wolfe Tone. It's not too great a stretch to suggest that Johnnie Fox's has been rebelling ever since— principally against seriousness. Because here, the emphasis is squarely on a good time, every time.

To describe the place as quirky would be a disservice to quirk. It's just bonkers. Wherever you look, there's all manner of bric-a-brac, memorabilia, curios, and knick-knacks—old signage, packaging, posters, ornaments, statues, and obscure paraphernalia.

The calm before the hooley.

trip, too. "There's no prima donnas, no special treatment here," laughs Tony. "All requests for privacy are politely declined. It's all for one and one for all!"

There is a very strong family vibe about the place. Many of the staff have been here for over twenty-five years. Tony himself is a local man who'd always hankered after an old country pub. When he got the chance to buy this one, he didn't think twice. "It's a work in progress," he says. "I'll never be done tinkering with the place."

Don't let the distance from Dublin put you off. There are, of course, shuttle buses that leave from the city center every evening, which means you've really no excuse for missing out on this extraordinary pub.

Is it the teeniest bit over-the-top? Maybe. A little. That's probably the point. But anyway, so what? The *craic* really is mighty up here.

Our best advice is, you can't fight the Fox. Just give in to the place. You'll enjoy the experience. The food is very good, the Guinness is excellent, and there's also a large range of craft beers. At present, you'll also find over fifty Irish whiskeys offered.

This is by definition a destination pub, with a large restaurant where every day they put on a full-scale live traditional music and Irish dancing show (the above-mentioned hooley). The restaurant itself specializes in seafood, which is brought in fresh every morning.

Johnnie Fox's is always busy, especially because of the restaurant and Hooley Show. But you can still enjoy a quiet pint in the bar by the turf fire—or even better, outside with a chaser of fresh Irish mountain air.

The owner is Tony McMahon, a man with a P. T. Barnum–style flair for promotion. Over the years he's organized all sorts of stunts to draw attention to his pub; and it's worked. Tourists—and, yes, locals—pack the place out every day. Many movie stars, rock stars, royalty, and presidents have made the

DUBLIN WHISKEY STORES AND MORE

The greater Dublin area offers several exceptionally fine stores specializing in all that the whiskey world has to offer—yes, even bottles from beyond these shores. Some of these outlets, such as Mitchell and Son, have more than one branch, which you should probably factor into any itinerary you're contemplating—you know, just to be thorough.

CELTIC WHISKEY SHOP & WINES ON THE GREEN

27-28 Dawson Street, Dublin 2
www.celticwhiskeyshop.com

Here it is, your every Christmas, birthday, rainy day, and because-I-deserve-it day, all rolled into one. For the whiskey lover, this truly is your happy place. The Celtic Whiskey Shop is Ireland's most-awarded such emporium (and we actually have several of them). You'll find the big names, the smaller names, and the practically microscopic; the Irish, the Scotch, the world whiskies, the rarities, and even some legends—you know, bottles you've only heard whispered about. Well, friend, the stories are true. Come in, take a look around. But you're going to need awhile.

MITCHELL AND SON WINE MERCHANTS

CHQ Building, IFSC, Docklands, Dublin 1
www.mitchellandson.com

The Mitchell family has been in the spirit trade for generations. More significantly, however, they are also the creators of the legendary Spot series of Irish whiskeys. Originally wine merchants, they would source pot still from Jameson's Bow Street distillery and then mature it in fortified wine casks. A system of colored "spots" (Green, Red, Blue, and Yellow) was introduced to indicate the age at which the whiskey would be ready to bottle. As many aficionados know, Green Spot is still around, of course, and Yellow Spot has recently been revived. We're still awaiting the returns of Red and Blue. In the meantime, there are plenty of remarkable whiskeys available in the stores. Yes, stores: There are two other locations— Glastule, County Dublin and Avoca in County Wicklow. It's good to be meticulous in life, so why not collect all three?

L. Mulligan Whiskey Shop

South William Street, Dublin 2
www.lmulliganwhiskeyshop.com

This is a smart new place, opened in
2016 by Michael Fogarty, formerly of
the Celtic Whiskey Shop, cofounder of
the Irish Whiskey Society, and co-owner
of the wonderful L. Mulligan Grocer.
All in all, that's quite a pedigree, and it
shows. The store has its own exclusive
Single Pot Still Powers in addition to
a breathtaking rare and collectible
selection. Well worth a visit.

THE JAMESON DISTILLERY BOW STREET

Smithfield Village, Dublin 7
www.jamesonwhiskey.com

Reopened in 2017 following a multi-
million-dollar investment program, the
home of one of the great names in Irish
whiskey has been transformed into an
extraordinary immersive experience for
everyone interested in the wonders of
uisce beatha.

The key to that experience is storytelling.
There are three fully guided tasting tours
on offer. The "Bow St. Experience" focuses
on Jameson's history and heritage, its
methods, and, of course, the famous
triple-distillation process that lends the
whiskey its exceptionally smooth finish.
The tour includes a comparative tasting
and a complimentary drink in the bar.

The "Whiskey Makers" tour is effectively
a master-class exploration of Jameson
Original and the three Whiskey Maker
series bottlings: Distiller's Safe, Cooper's
Croze, and Blender's Dog. There's a
tasting guide to explain ingredients and
flavor profiles, and you'll even be given

the chance to create your own
blend. The tour includes the
maturation warehouse, where
you get the opportunity to
sample Jameson straight from
the cask.

"Whiskey Shakers" is, yes,
all about cocktails—history,
ingredients, and recipes, all
featuring Jameson, of course.
Then it's time to get hands-
on with all the professional
bar tools and ingredients and
make your own version of a
classic whiskey cocktail. This
tour also finishes with a visit
to the maturation warehouse
and a sample or two from
selected casks.

All three tours are offered
seven days a week, but numbers
for each are strictly limited, so
arrive a little early if you can.

THE COUNTIES OF
MUNSTER

Clare
Cork
Kerry
Limerick
Tipperary
Waterford

VISITING MUNSTER

OK, LET'S ESTABLISH SOME PARAMETERS. HOW
LONG HAVE YOU GOT? OH NO, NO, NO—YOU'D
NEED MORE THAN THAT FOR KERRY ALONE.
SOME OF OUR GREATEST HITS ARE HERE IN THE
PLACE THEY CALL THE KINGDOM, LIKE THE
LAKES OF KILLARNEY. AND THEY REALLY ARE AS
BREATHTAKING AS YOU'VE ALWAYS HEARD.

Kerry is home to the highest mountain range in Ireland, and a lot of the county seems to be either soaring peaks, endless valleys, or stunning beaches.

There are numerous scenic drives mapped out for you, or take an organized tour of the Ring of Kerry and the Dingle Peninsula. There are also boat trips out to the Blasket Islands, the remote, mystical archipelago that survived as an outpost of ancient Ireland until the 1950s.

County Clare has the Cliffs of Moher—a genuinely unforgettable sight. You'll feel you're standing at the edge of the universe, a dizzying seven hundred feet above the crashing Atlantic waves, with seagulls being buffeted about far, far below you. Amazing.

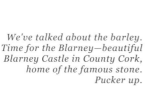

We've talked about the barley.
Time for the Blarney—beautiful
Blarney Castle in County Cork,
home of the famous stone.
Pucker up.

Munster has truly spectacular scenery, and plenty of it.

Also in Clare is the otherworldly Burren—an extraordinary limestone pavement that extends for miles and miles. It's home to a particularly varied and protected ecosystem, with lots of rare plants growing in the fissures. Try to imagine a lunar landscape with butterflies. A definite must-see.

In Ireland—where we produce so much of the stuff—even we acknowledge that there's more to life than scenery. There are an enormous number of craft and artisan producers in Munster, creating everything from perfumes, crystal, and jewelry to handmade chocolates, woolens, and ceramics. Cork and Limerick have high-end department stores and boutiques, while if you're looking for restaurants, well, take your pick. The quality of the seafood alone is worth the price of admission. And as for nightlife, ask anyone. They'll have a suggestion or ten for you, and they'll all be good. All you'll have to do is find the place. Now, are you sure you've left enough time? You can always get another flight, you know . . .

The Neolithic Poulnabrone portal tomb in the Burren.

A SHORT HISTORY OF DISTILLING IN MUNSTER

Munster and Midleton, Midleton and Munster: When we come to consider the history of whiskey-making in the region, we simply can't separate the two.

Midleton is of course an anchor to the past, to the halcyon, rip-roaring golden age when Irish pot still was king of the world. Even in the latter half of the twentieth century, when the entire industry appeared to be tottering toward oblivion, it was still a presence—a glimmer in the dark. And it's here now, preserving the best of the great tradition while continuing to forge a dynamic new one.

In the heyday of Irish whiskey (of licensed, legal distilling, that is), Midleton was just one of a number of big producers in the region. In the late nineteenth century, Cork city alone supported seven substantial makers. Limerick, too, had a sizeable industry. In Kerry, Clare, and Tipperary the tradition was more artisanal, less industrialized.

Today, all manner of things are happening in Munster whiskey, from family farms seeking to diversify their activities to innovative large-scale spirit producers. In Chapel Gate, County Clare, the business is not whiskey-distilling, it's whiskey bonding—reviving an almost-forgotten component of the Irish whiskey story. In Waterford Distillery, Mark Reynier is taking the concepts of provenance and terroir to degrees of sophistication the Irish industry has never seen. In West Cork Distillery, a former industrial chemist and two boyhood friends from a tiny village have hand-built a facility that is producing significant volumes of whiskey, as well as gin and vodka.

And of course, there's Midleton. Some of the best Irish whiskeys ever made came from here; and they still do today.

The story of whiskey-making in Munster isn't just two chapters—an illustrious history followed by a dynamic, resurgent present. There's real continuity here, through the ups and downs. You might think that sound you're hearing is the heartbeat of the Irish whiskey industry, but another way to look at it is to call it what it is: the unceasing soundtrack of malting, milling, mashing, fermentation, distillation, maturation, and bottling. Which is where the rest of us gleefully come in.

MUNSTER
DISTILLERIES
OF TODAY

If you listen quietly, you can hear
the angels claiming their share . . .

WATERFORD DISTILLERY

THE SIGN SAYS, "WHERE BARLEY IS KING, PROVENANCE
IS ALL." AND THEY REALLY MEAN IT. FOR THIS IS
PROVENANCE ELEVATED TO A DEGREE UNKNOWN
IN IRISH DISTILLING, AND MATCHED ONLY BY THE
AMBITION BEHIND IT.

Grattan Quay
Waterford
County Waterford

www.waterforddistillery.ie

THE PROVINCE OF
MUNSTER

*Provenance and terroir: Here, they distill
using the barley from only one farm at a time.*

At Waterford they have sourced barley from around sixty Irish farms, including several run on organic and biodynamic principles. The harvests come from some nineteen distinct soil types. All of this information is logged in a digital tracking system— along with the name of the farmer, the exact GPS location of the farm, and a great deal more data. Because here, data is distillation. Each farmer's barley is stored separately and distilled separately. This week, they're distilling only the crop from Farm A. Next week, only the barley from Farm B, and so on.

Each bottle from Waterford Distillery will therefore carry the name of the farmer that planted the seed that tended the crop that harvested the barley that made the whisky. (More on that spelling of whiskey later.)

The impressive atrium has a map showing all the suppliers and their details. What's more, all of this information is available 24/7 on their extraordinarily comprehensive website. You can track whose barley is going through the distillery today, the soil type that produced it, as well as the

MUNSTER *DISTILLERIES OF TODAY*

name and location of the farm. There are video portraits of the farmers to watch. Why? "Because we've nothing to hide," says head distiller Ned Gahan. But it's more than that. It's that all-important provenance thing again.

Each farmer supplies one hundred metric tons of barley, of which seventy-five go to the maltings. No enzymes are used in the malting process and no gibberelic acid (which is commonly used in distilling to modify grains). At Waterford they don't want to change the profile of the grains. They use a mash filter rather than a Lauter tun. "It improves yield because it produces more sugars for the yeast to consume," says Ned. And nothing will be added at bottling. The whisky will be what it is, nothing more, nothing less. And, they say, the goal is "the world's most profound single malt."

The art they practice here is to take three simple ingredients— barley, yeast, and water—push them as far as possible and also as naturally as possible. That involves extraordinary investment, dedication, and technology. But for all the evident wizardry at Waterford, at heart this is a profoundly traditional approach to distilling, a return to ancient ways of handling grain that ensures it is pure and unadulterated—just as it's supposed to be. In a way, it's akin to the micro-distilling approach of the old *poitín*-makers but scaled up to the macro level.

Fifty percent of each farm's double-distilled spirit goes into first-fill ex-bourbon casks, 20 percent into virgin oak, 15 percent into premium French wine casks (e.g., Mouton Rothschild Lafite), and the remainder into fortified wine casks such as port, sherry, or Madeira. What's more, where most distillers will finish their whiskey for, say, six months in a port cask, Waterford turns this orthodoxy on its head and will age its whisky for three to five years in a port cask. The reason? "Flavor."

"You see, we're not a typical distillery," offers Ned, with no hint of irony, "but our philosophy is unique." The distillery was originally a state-of-the-art brewery built by Diageo in 2004. It operated

The stills—from Inverleven to Waterford.

in this guise for around ten years; then the beer production was shifted elsewhere and the plant was shuttered.

When Waterford Distillery founder Mark Reynier found the building, he negotiated some of the equipment as part of the acquisition from Diageo. The stills themselves were sourced from Bruichladdich, where Mark was formerly CEO. Originally the stills were used at Inverleven. However, for years afterward the spirit still languished outside in a yard at Port Charlotte, while the wash still sat unused beside the Bruichladdich distillery.

Mark's background in Scotch distilling is where his obsession with provenance first took root. His experience of viticulture also led to his discovery of biodynamic principles, which have been established in wine-making for many years, though not commonly applied in the world of *uisce beatha*. His preference for "whisky" rather than "whiskey" harks back to the original Irish spelling. There's that obsession with authenticity again.

There is no rush to market here. Spirit is being laid down. Casks are stacking up. The angels are going about their larcenous work. Time is passing. It'll keep passing; it always does. And the world will wait for Waterford whisky until Waterford whisky says when. And not a moment sooner.

AT A GLANCE

FIRST DISTILLATION
2016

STILLS
2 Pot Stills (Wash Still: 24,000L, Spirit Still: 17,000L)

LPA
1 million

WHISKEY STYLES
Single Malt

VISITOR CENTER/TOURS
No/by apppointment only

123

MUNSTER *DISTILLERIES OF TODAY*

MIDLETON DISTILLERY

IT'S OFTEN SAID OF THE INGREDIENTS FOR MAKING IRISH WHISKEY THAT TIME IS THE MOST IMPORTANT. AND IT IS. HOWEVER, THERE'S ANOTHER WAY OF LOOKING AT THE MATTER OF TIME IN RELATION TO WHISKEY, AND THAT'S LONGEVITY.

Distillery Walk
Midleton
County Cork

www.jamesonwhiskey.com
www.singlepotstill.com

THE PROVINCE OF
MUNSTER

A long history is never a question of mere luck. It's the product of skill, ingenuity, perhaps a degree of cunning—and yes, maybe a little luck, too. Which brings us to Midleton, the history of which could fill an entire bookshelf and still not exhaust the subject. Our interest is in Midleton today, but that does require a quick look over the shoulder at yesterday.

Founded in 1825, this distillery was built for volume. By 1830 it was producing some 400,000 gallons (1.6 million liters) of whiskey a year. It employed over two hundred people and was intimately linked to the local agricultural economy. The world's largest pot still was here, with a capacity of over 31,000 gallons (140,000 liters), in addition to two 10,000-gallon (45,000-liter) spirit stills.

Along with Belfast, Dublin, and, to a lesser extent, Derry and Limerick, Midleton was one of the cornerstones of the Irish distilling industry in its golden age, during the late eighteenth and nineteenth centuries.

The mighty Midleton stills: busier than ever.

This meant it suffered the same fate as the others in the economic maelstrom of the early/mid-twentieth century brought about by Prohibition in the United States, civil war at home, two world wars, and a trade war with Britain.

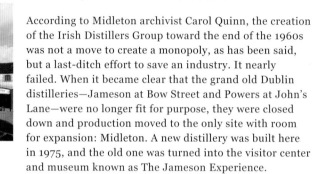

According to Midleton archivist Carol Quinn, the creation of the Irish Distillers Group toward the end of the 1960s was not a move to create a monopoly, as has been said, but a last-ditch effort to save an industry. It nearly failed. When it became clear that the grand old Dublin distilleries—Jameson at Bow Street and Powers at John's Lane—were no longer fit for purpose, they were closed down and production moved to the only site with room for expansion: Midleton. A new distillery was built here in 1975, and the old one was turned into the visitor center and museum known as The Jameson Experience.

Production focused initially on Jameson, the brand with the greatest international potential—and as such, deemed to offer the best chance of survival. Names such as Powers, Paddy, and Midleton's own range took a back seat.

In 1988 Irish Distillers merged with Pernod-Ricard, which gave the Cork distillery access to a vast global distribution network, and helped consolidate Jameson as the world's largest-selling Irish whiskey.

In addition, this new commercial clout enabled Midleton to revive those old brands along with Tullamore D.E.W., Redbreast, and the famous Spot series (Green Spot and Yellow Spot); to develop new ranges; and to create premium extensions to its core Jameson, Powers, and Midleton portfolios. The distillery has also continued to innovate with blends, maturation, and cask wood—including, recently, chestnut and Irish oak.

Today Midleton effectively operates two stillhouses—the Barry Crockett, named in honor of its legendary distiller emeritus, and the Garden Still House. The two share the same milling, mashing, and brewing facilities, and run identical stills. Brian Nation, the head distiller, manages both operations. They use a mash filter rather than a Lauter tun. "It improves yield because it produces more sugars for the yeast to consume," explains Brian.

The Garden Still House, which opened in 2013.

Following expansion in 2012, the grain distillery now features six columns: two sets of beer, extraction, and rectifiers. In 2013 Midleton opened its Whiskey Academy to train bar industry professionals about the world of *uisce beatha*. It also has a separate experimental or micro distillery, headed by Henry Donnelly, where distilling graduates of the academy can fine-tune their skills. This is a testing ground for innovation, for experimenting with mashbills, and serves as a platform for the distillery's Method and Madness range.

And so, once again, longevity is protected, preserved—and ensured. It was just a matter of time.

AT A GLANCE

FIRST DISTILLATION
1975

STILLS
10 Pot Stills each with 80,000L capacity located at Barry Crockett (6 stills) and Garden Still House (4 Stills)
6 Column Stills
3 Pot Stills at the Micro Distillery

LPA
Over 60 million

WHISKEY STYLES
Single Malt, Pot Still & Grain

VISITOR CENTER/TOURS
Yes and Irish Whiskey Academy

KEY BOTTLINGS

JAMESON: ORIGINAL; CASKMATES IPA AND STOUT EDITIONS; BLACK BARREL, CRESTED 10

REDBREAST: 12-,15-, AND 21-YEAR-OLDS; LUSTAU SHERRY FINISH; CASK STRENGTH

GREEN SPOT AND YELLOW SPOT

MIDLETON: LEGACY; DAIR GAELACH; VERY RARE

POWERS: GOLD LABEL; JOHN'S LANE 12 SIGNATURE, THREE SWALLOW

METHOD AND MADNESS RANGE

CLONAKILTY DISTILLERY

THE SCULLY FAMILY HAS BEEN FARMING THIS SEA-SWEPT LAND ON THE COAST OF WEST CORK FOR EIGHT GENERATIONS. NO, THAT'S NOT QUITE RIGHT. THEY HAVE BEEN GUARDIANS—STEWARDS OF THIS LAND FOR EIGHT GENERATIONS. THEY FEEL A TRUE RESPONSIBILITY TOWARD IT.

The Waterfront
Clonakilty
County Cork

www.clonakiltydistillery.ie

THE PROVINCE OF
MUNSTER

Fine Irish whiskey. Where else?
On the rocks.

C onsequently, the idea for a whiskey and gin distillery is intrinsically linked to this intense relationship with the land. The barley is theirs—ancient varieties that the family has revived. The water is theirs, too—drawn cold and pure from deep rock strata beneath their fields adjacent to the base of Galley Head Lighthouse. The gin that the distillery aims to produce will feature botanicals foraged from the seashore. As founder Michael Scully puts it, "It was a matter of taking what we have on our doorstep and simply joining the dots."

The distillery itself was still under construction at the time we visited. The building—actually a former bank—is something of a landmark in this seaside town, with an expansive glass frontage offering dramatic views over the water. There is even salt spray on the windows. The building has a large courtyard, which will eventually be developed into an alfresco dining and entertainment space. The courtyard is also home to a striking sculpture of a minke whale diving back beneath the waves.

Few distilleries have a statue of a minke whale outside. This one does.

This is the symbol of the Clonakilty Distillery brand. The whales are often spotted off the coast here, and the sculpture provides a powerful, visible link to the vital sense of place that pervades everything about this distillery.

Clonakilty already has spirit laid down, a triple-distilled single malt maturing in ex-bourbon barrels, before being finished in port casks. In the meantime, it has so far offered two grain-malt blends finished in either virgin American oak or port casks. (Both are ABV 43.6 percent and non-chill-filtered.)

The warehouse is off-site but still nearby on the Atlantic coast. Michael believes the cool sea air drifting around the barrels and interacting with the wood imparts a distinctive maritime character to the maturing whiskey.

Plans for the visitor center are ambitious, promising "an immersive sensory experience," with several levels of tour on offer. There'll also be a full restaurant on-site, showcasing the best of local produce. This is yet another example of terroir put into practice in the runaway renaissance of Irish whiskey. We're excited to see how those first casks turn out. But we'll have to be patient—because you can't rush nature. Just ask any farmer.

Two fanboys and founder Michael Scully, center.

AT A GLANCE

FIRST DISTILLATION
2018 (expected)

STILLS
3 Pot Stills (Wash Still: 7,500L, Intermediate Still: 4,600L, Spirit Still 4,600L)

LPA
350,000 projected

WHISKEY STYLES
Single Pot Still

VISITOR CENTER/TOURS
Yes

WEST CORK DISTILLERS

"IT'S ABSOLUTE MADNESS." JOHN O'CONNELL HAS A CLEAR MEMORY OF HIS MOTHER'S REACTION WHEN HE TOLD HER HE WAS LEAVING A VERY SUCCESSFUL CAREER IN FOOD RESEARCH AND DEVELOPMENT TO START, OF ALL THINGS, A DISTILLERY. AND DID HE KNOW MUCH ABOUT DISTILLING AT THE TIME? "NO, NOT EXACTLY."

Marsh Road
Skibbereen
County Cork

www.westcorkdistillers.com

THE PROVINCE OF
MUNSTER

They needed a distillery, so they made one.

Ⅰt got worse. He was going to start this business with two of his oldest friends, cousins Dennis and Ger McCarthy. They knew even less about distilling than John. However, and this is important, setting up West Cork Distillers was no shot in the dark—precisely because of the three personalities involved.

The three of them grew up together in a tiny West Cork fishing village (population circa 120). After school, John went off to university and the cousins went off to sea. While he got a PhD in colloidal chemistry and worked in multinationals, they labored on the trawlers for fifteen long years. By the time the cousins had saved enough to buy their own boat, the Irish fishing industry was collapsing around them. Things were looking grim. One day they got talking to their old friend about what their next move should be. And as it happened, John had an idea.

John is a scientist to the tips of his fingers. Dennis and Ger are workhorses to the ends of theirs. Together, they physically constructed the workings of the distillery—including the very pot stills themselves, as well as almost all of the fermentation and mashing equipment. That can-do attitude is everywhere here. If something is needed, they make it. There is even a dedicated fabrication workshop on-site, and you get the strong impression that the three founders know every bolt, rivet, valve, gasket, and thingamajig in the place.

Founder John O'Connell in his lab.

Which is not to suggest for a moment that West Cork Distillers is some kind of fantastical, cobbled-together Rube Goldberg contraption. Nothing could be further from the truth. The distillery is immaculate, logical, professional, and state-of-the-art. They employ a full-time software engineer just to write code to manage operations. John has two chromatographs and a spectrometer he uses to analyze the grain, yeast, and yield every day. "Science is important," he says. "It's God's law." And, presumably, using technology to control the things that can be controlled leaves more room in the whiskey equation for the other stuff—the mystery and magic.

The main pot still is known as The Rocket and is, John claims, the fastest in the world. The flow plate is also, apparently, the largest in the country. These points are not made in order to brag. For John O'Connell they're simply evidence of successfully applied technology. "That's what drives the company," he says.

The building itself is a former fish processing plant, where all three founders once worked during their school vacations. Now they employ around fifty local people, mostly ex-fisherman. There is no dedicated sales staff. The distillery's location in West Cork's famously mild microclimate makes it ideal, says John, for the maturation of fine Irish whiskey. To which the only logical response is: QED.

At WCD, as the company refers to itself, they use only local Irish grain and untreated spring water, brought in from a source a couple of miles away. They also malt some of their own barley on-site.

Jack, the barrel-whisperer, having a private moment.

The distillery's foundation on the empirical method is not restrictive. So experimentation is an essential part of life here. In addition to the usual cask finishes of bourbon, sherry, port, and rum, West Cork is looking at using cognac, Calvados, and even sake barrels. For their Black Cask blend the team developed some new technology for charring the barrels using a flame fueled by peat, rather than the standard gas flame. All of the whiskey is triple-distilled, and the award-winning range includes Bourbon Cask, a 3:1 grain/malt blend; a ten-year-old single malt; and the above-mentioned Black Cask, a 2:1 grain/malt blend finished in double-charred casks. There is also Pogues, "the official whiskey of the legendary band."

As well as the West Cork whiskey lines, WCD produces the Two Trees brand, which includes a gin, a vodka, and a quadruple-distilled *poitín*. There's another gin brand, Garnish Island. The company has its own wholesale and distribution arm. It also does all its own bottling on-site. As yet, they aren't actually manufacturing the glass for the bottles—but if anyone can . . .

AT A GLANCE

FIRST DISTILLATION
2008

STILLS
5 Pot Stills

LPA
3 million

WHISKEY STYLES
Single Malt & Pot Still

VISITOR CENTER/TOURS
No

KEY BOTTLINGS

BOURBON CASK 10-YEAR-OLD SINGLE MALT
ABV: 40%

BOURBON CASK 12-YEAR-OLD SINGLE MALT
ABV: 43%—a limited release finished variously in rum, sherry, or port casks

BLACK CASK BLENDED IRISH WHISKEY
ABV: 40%

MUNSTER DISTILLERIES OF TODAY

Blink and you'll miss it: the superfast Rocket still, left.

CATHAL
BR
DINGLE
COUNTY KERRY
WHISKEY DISTILLERY
Ireland
FOUNDING FATHERS
GREG
DAVID C
BRIAN TUOHY

DINGLE WHISKEY DISTILLERY

PLANS FOR MOST NEW DISTILLERY VENTURES BEGIN IN A GIDDY MIXTURE OF HOPE AND OPTIMISM. IN THE CASE OF DINGLE, IT WAS MORE AKIN TO UTTER BLIND FAITH.

*Farranredmond
Dingle
County Kerry*

www.dingledistillery.ie

THE PROVINCE OF
MUNSTER

For this was 2009, when Ireland was still in the grim grip of recession. "On the face of it, not a great time to be thinking about something like this," concedes director Elliot Hughes, son of the late Oliver Hughes (who cofounded the groundbreaking Porterhouse craft brewing group). Yet that blind faith proved well-founded. The distillery began operating fully in 2012, and today is at the forefront of a new generation of artisan Irish whiskey distillers, winning awards, building a reputation, and gaining enthusiastic customers at home and overseas.

There are several reasons for its success. For one thing, at Dingle they started small and—unlike most businesses—harbor no plans to become a megabrand. Elliot is up front about his goal for the distillery: "We want to establish ourselves as a niche producer of extraordinary single malts." Modest, yet ambitious at the same time, they have retained an unwavering focus on quality and flavor. Nothing is released until it's more than good enough.

A tribute to those who have bought a cask—and helped secure the distillery's future.

These Irish whiskey stills have an exceptional pedigree: Scotch.

At Dingle they have three copper pot stills for their whiskey, designed by Scotch expert John MacDougall. There is also a small swan-neck still used for gin and vodka. It's called Oisin, after the great poet of Irish legend and son of the mighty Finn McCool. There is no column still, so the distillery's gin and vodka are made with third-party neutral spirit. The barley for the whiskey comes from Cork and is milled in Kilkenny. The water is from the distillery's own well.

John MacDougall's design of the stills incorporates a boil ball into the neck, which, it's claimed, boosts reflux and produces a markedly smoother spirit. Another distinguishing feature is the wooden fermentation vessels that are used. There is very little automation in the distillery. A lot of work is done by hand, which provides employment for local people. Warehousing is also managed on-site.

With so much hands-on activity, job descriptions are, well, fluid. Master distiller Michael Walsh says his day can involve anything from managing operations and monitoring the stills to shifting five-hundred-liter barrels, or handpicking local botanicals for Dingle's unique gin bottlings (which are based around the four seasons). Michael also personally conducts a couple of the tour visits a week. There is no visitor center as such. However, visitors do get to experience a working distillery up close.

A striking feature of the distillery is the Founding Fathers' Wall of Names. A stack of wooden slabs from floor to ceiling carries the names of all five hundred who have bought a cask (or two)—and thereby helped ensure the independence of the business.

The town itself is very supportive and proud of the distillery. There are enthusiastic, unofficial ambassadors for the Dingle brand everywhere. Go into any pub—there are quite a few—and you'll find local people ordering Dingle whiskey, gin, and vodka. Because it belongs to the town. It's theirs.

Fanboy Tim and Dingle director Elliot Hughes.

The logo for Dingle Distillery is a Wren Boy holding a sheaf of wheat. The reference is to a centuries-old rural tradition, when men disguised in a straw costume would tour the area on the 26th of December, cheeping and squawking like wrens to scare away evil spirits. The practice is still observed around here, though it's safe to say the only spirits left are good ones. Very, very good ones.

AT A GLANCE

FIRST DISTILLATION
2012

STILLS
3 Pot Stills

LPA
2 casks per day

WHISKEY STYLES
Single Malt & Grain

VISITOR CENTER/TOURS
No

KEY BOTTLINGS

DINGLE SINGLE MALT
ABV: 46.5%

Wooden fermentation vessels: another unusual feature.

CHAPEL GATE IRISH WHISKEY CO.

THE RENAISSANCE IN IRISH WHISKEY DISTILLING IS FULL OF MAVERICK SOULS, CHARACTERS WHO HAVE SEIZED AN OPPORTUNITY TO DO THINGS THEIR WAY, DAMMIT. THEIR WAY CAN MEAN ANYTHING FROM HIGH-TECH TO DEFIANTLY LOW-TECH, FROM A RETURN TO TRADITIONAL METHODS TO AN INNOVATIVE APPROACH TO INGREDIENTS, SAY, OR LEFT-FIELD CASKING METHODS.

Gowerhass
Cooraclare
Kilrush, County Clare

www.chapelgatewhiskey.com

THE PROVINCE OF
MUNSTER

A nd in the case of Louise McGuane of Chapel Gate Distillery, it means something else again: a revival of the lost art of whiskey bonding.

There hasn't been a licensed whiskey bonder in Ireland for over fifty years (or for that matter, a licensed whiskey-maker in County Clare in more than a century either). Yet, right up until the industrialization of the distilling industry in the nineteenth century, bonding was standard practice. Traders would bring their own barrels to the distiller, fill them, and then bring the whiskey home to their farm or pub. They were then responsible for maturing the whiskey, blending, diluting it from cask strength, and bottling it. When bonding was the norm, the flavor of the whiskey was always local—specific to the place where it matured. When bonding vanished, Louise believes, so too did true variety of flavor in Irish whiskey.

For that reason, at Chapel Gate they didn't build a distillery on the family farm. They built a barn. But not just any barn: a whiskey rackhouse, with

Sometimes innovation starts by looking back . . .

a loose earthen floor to regulate humidity. The farm, located on the Wild Atlantic Way, enjoys a microclimate of briny air and frequent fluctuations in barometric pressure and temperature. All of this was taken into account in the design and orientation of the rackhouse, in order to give the maturing whiskey every chance.

The farm, located on the Wild Atlantic Way . . .

The barrels are stored "on the bilge" here, meaning on their sides, rather than stacked vertically as is the norm. Louise contends that the extra contact between the whiskey and both heads of the barrel will benefit the flavor extraction. She's a firm believer that 80 percent of whiskey flavor comes from a combination of the wood in which it ages, and the climate around it. "But we have to wait a few years to see if we're right," she says.

All of the spirit is new-make grain and malt whiskey, distilled to Louise's specification. A drinks industry veteran, she knows exactly what she's looking for. And it's already paying off. Chapel Gate's premium blend, The Gael, has won acclaim at both the World Spirits Awards and Irish Whiskey Awards. The whiskey is matured in Grade A ex-bourbon barrels that Louise sources herself in Kentucky.

The Gael is named after, of all things, a bicycle invented by a local nineteenth-century bonder and all-round entrepreneur, J.J. Corry. Louise discovered J.J.'s story when researching the history of Irish bonding. The inspiration she was looking for turned out to be from just down the road from the family farm—in Kilrush.

Louise calls herself a blender, not a distiller. For her, whiskey bonding allows Chapel Gate to be completely transparent about its whiskey, in a way that many distillers simply can't be. "What I'm really excited about is having a library of fantastic Irish whiskeys from all over the county in about five years," she says. "It's a very long game," she concedes. "But we think it'll be worth the wait."

The traditional rackhouse, where Chapel Gate matures its whiskey "on the bilge."

AT A GLANCE

RACKHOUSE CAPACITY
350-400 casks, with a second rackhouse planned

VISITOR CENTER/TOURS
By appointment

KEY BOTTLINGS

J.J. CORRY THE GAEL
ABV: 46%

Louise reminds a barrel just who's in charge around here.

MUNSTER'S
GREAT IRISH PUBS

A well-used snug: the best kind.

JIM O' THE MILL

Upperchurch
Thurles
County Tipperary

THE PROVINCE OF
MUNSTER

FIRST, A QUESTION. CAN YOU GET TO
UPPERCHURCH FROM WHEREVER YOU ARE IN
THE WORLD BY NEXT THURSDAY EVENING?
IF SO, THEN DO. LEAVE NOW. BECAUSE
THERE YOU'LL FIND A PUB THAT'S BEEN
CALLED THE BEST IN THE WORLD . . .

A pub *The Irish Times* named the best in the country in 2015. A pub with one solitary beer tap. A pub that only opens once a week—on Thursday evening.

People come from all over not so much to drink here as to experience here. For what happens every Thursday at Jim O' The Mill is nothing short of an event—a shared celebration of song, story, *craic*, and neighborliness that's been called the beating heart of Irishness.

The pub itself is a converted mill dating back to around 1820. It still has the original flagged stone floors and a couple of open fires. It also has the Ryan family—Jim and Kaye and their five musical daughters, Róisín, Áine, Greta, Cáit, and Erin. This is their home. On Thursday evenings, they open it to the world. And the world flocks here to talk and laugh, to sing and play, or just to listen and be glad in this giddy vortex of joy.

Jim O' The Mill doesn't look like a pub from the outside. There are no brewery signs or branded materials of any kind. It looks like what it is: a pretty-as-a-picture farmhouse cradled in the hollow of a hill. As they say around here, it's easy to find if you know where it is. But if you need help, ask to be pointed toward the metal bridge and make your way from there.

Many pubs have been called the best in Ireland. But late into the night, with Friday morning just peeping around the corner, when you're eating Kaye's hot, freshly made wheaten bread with salty local butter, when the music feels like it's about to lift the roof and take you with it, you'll think to yourself: This might just be the one.

*The pub itself
is a converted
mill dating back
to around 1820 . . .*

Hear that? It's the beating heart of Irishness.

*There's only one beer on tap. Nobody seems to mind the limited choice
very much.*

McCARTHY'S HOTEL

Main Street
Spitalfield, Fethard
County Tipperary

www.mccarthyshotel.net

MANY OF THE PUBS FEATURED IN THIS BOOK WERE ONCE SPIRIT GROCERS. A FEW DO STILL CARRY ON A LITTLE NON-PUB TRADE, LIKE HARDWARE OR FARM SUPPLIES. BUT ONLY ONE COMBINES A PUB AND THE LOCAL UNDERTAKER'S.

THE PROVINCE OF
MUNSTER

McCARTHY'S HOTEL

For publican Vinny Murphy—known to everyone as Jasper for reasons that aren't quite clear—it's just the family business. He grew up with it and, yes, he's heard all the jokes: "He's the man who put the spirit into spirit grocer. Things have gone from bad to hearse . . ." And so on. It's water off a duck's back.

Over the years, many wakes have been held here, and you can certainly imagine worse places to say *slán*—farewell.

The McCarthy name has been over the door since the mid-nineteenth century, when the place also included a bakery, a hardware store, a livery stable, a draper, and a hotel. (It's still sometimes referred to locally as a hotel, but, much as you might want to, you can't actually spend the night here. Unless you're a customer of the other side of the business, that is.)

Jasper Murphy: He's heard 'em all . . .

A fine place to contemplate the meaning of life and what we call the afterlife—you know, closing time.

The interior hasn't really changed in over a century. It's got the same wooden floor, same shelves, same snugs, same counter, and same warm hospitality. Continuity is a grand thing for the living as well as the late.

Fethard is a small village with medieval bones. That makes it a place of interest for history buffs. This part of Tipperary is serious horse country, too, which brings a different type of connoisseur to the pub. McCarthy's gets plenty of celebrity visitors, as well. A well-known peer of the British theater owns a castle nearby, but no one thinks twice about seeing him around the place, says Jasper. However, one notorious American goth rocker wasn't convinced. When he got married in a local castle in 2005, there was a request to bring the wedding party to McCarthy's—on condition that the locals vacated the bar. Jasper politely declined. "Sure no one would have bothered him at all—you know, unless he said something bad about the Tipperary senior hurling team." Absolutely. Everyone has their limits.

J&K WALSH
Spirit Grocer

11 Great George's Street
Waterford
County Waterford

SOME PUBS GET RENOVATED. SOME GET
REFURBISHED. A FEW GET RESTORED. AND
THEN, ONCE IN A VERY BLUE MOON, ONE
GETS RESURRECTED. LIKE J&K WALSH.

When Michael Watchorn bought the pub a couple of years ago, it was in a pretty bad way. The previous owner, a blind man who lived upstairs, had run it alone (which is a story in itself). But as soon as he stood in the doorway, Michael saw the potential. "The essence of something magical from another era was still there," he recalls. Many of the original features and fittings—the drawers and shelves, etc.—had deteriorated badly and were in pieces, and so Michael had them remade by local craftsmen. There were structural problems. The place needed to be replumbed, rewired, reborn. But slowly, slowly, that magical thing that Michael first glimpsed began to reappear.

It's said that a good pub will take you out of yourself, but a great one will take you out of time. Well, that's what's waiting for you here.

Superior woodwork, superior pub: It's axiomatic.

In JK's, as everyone calls it, that time is somewhere around the late 1890s, give or take. Now, there are of course a few concessions to modernity. The glassware is authentic 1950s and the shiny new beer taps are from the 1960s—when draft beer arrived in Ireland. That's as newfangled as it gets here.

There are only three taps because Michael reckons that's plenty. There is a good choice of bottled beers and a fine whiskey selection. What's more, JK's also has a comfortable snug—always a plus—where you can talk to the smartly dressed bar staff through a serving hatch. So you don't even have to get up from your seat.

Understandably, there is no TV here, no Wi-Fi, and no music. Just conversation, *craic*, and laughter. Twenty-first century, eat your heart out.

MARY KENNEDY'S

Callaghane
Grantstown
County Waterford

YES, IT'S REAL. THIS LONG, LOW,
CREAMY-COLORED THATCHED COTTAGE IS A
PUB—AND UNQUESTIONABLY A GREAT ONE.
WHAT'S MORE, THE BEAUTIFUL EXTERIOR
IS A GOOD INDICATION OF WHAT'S INSIDE.

THE PROVINCE OF
MUNSTER

The house itself has been on the site here in Grantstown since the 1700s and has been licensed since the late 1800s. Outside, you can still see the hoops where customers would tether their horses and donkeys. Five generations of Kennedys have run the place, and today it is in the hands of the formidable Mary K. She started helping out her uncle around the place many years ago when she was a girl. When his health declined, she stayed on, and on.

Mary's pub is comfortable and warm, with a big open fire fed from a basket of turf and sticks. It is also utterly immaculate. (You get the impression Mary is as unlikely to tolerate a speck of dust as a request to see the cocktail menu.) This being horse country, there are images of famous winners and jockeys about the place, along with clippings of local GAA glories, and so on. The quirkiest thing is probably the chandelier. It used to be a cartwheel. A large wall clock loudly chimes the half hour.

There's a music *seisiún* here on the second Thursday of the month. It's an informal thing, with the tunes passed around the room, in the old style. So if you're bursting to give a song or play an air, bide your time. Your turn will come.

There's no extravagant selection of rare whiskeys or other spirits here. Mary sticks to the classics. She also serves a very fine pint of Guinness ("a very short draw—that's the secret!"). And she makes you feel very, very welcome. "You must always make people feel at home," insists Mary. "That's the most important thing of all." It's also, we'd say, the very soul of greatness.

*Five generations
of Kennedys have
run the place . . .*

As lovely on the outside as it is on the inside.

JACK MEADE'S

Cheekpoint
Waterford
County Waterford
www.jackmeades.com

THE PROVINCE OF
MUNSTER

CALL IT LUCK, CALL IT FATE, CALL IT THE
WILL OF THE UNIVERSE, BUT SOMETHING,
SOMEWHERE IS ON THIS PUB'S SIDE. IT
SHOULDN'T HAVE SURVIVED THIS LONG. BUT
IT DID, AND IT WILL CONTINUE TO SURVIVE.

Firstly, the exterior tells you that there's definitely a tale here. The pub is jammed up against a viaduct. No, that's not quite it. In 1860 a viaduct was built across the place. (A sign outside reads: "Ireland's only flyover pub!") As the story goes, the original house, which was part of a famine village, was due to be demolished to make way for a nearby flour mill. The tenants refused to leave and, remarkably for those days, a judge upheld their claim, ordering that they could remain and the viaduct be built around the house.

The building itself dates back to the early 1700s. The Meade family took it over in 1857, when it was known as Halfway House and was a post office as well as a pub. They soon added some other buildings in the back—limekilns and an icehouse— and the business prospered, give or take the occasional flooding from the river running alongside. However, by the 1960s, it had shut its doors, apparently for good.

And then Willie Hartley and his wife, Carmel—coincidentally, the daughter of Jack Meade himself—bought it. Willie was a local agricultural contractor. This meant he had access to the machinery needed to do the reclamation work to shore up the back and put a stop to the flooding—among many other essential tasks. "Otherwise, sure I wouldn't have taken it on," Willie admits.

But he's glad he did. The spirit of the original pub remains intact, and the ancient flagstone floor and timbered ceiling are still here, along with the fine old fireplace. It's a cozy, good-time spot. But that's not all. Jack Meade's is now a complex, with an extensive beer garden and large, modern secondary bar, restaurant, and banquet hall. There's a river walk, a children's play area, and even a petting zoo. If the emphasis in what's called the Old Bar is on an authentic, traditional Irish pub experience, the rest of the place is focused on family entertainment and dining. "You've got to adapt to survive," says Willie, with the air of a man who knows exactly what he's talking about, and has the pub to prove it.

The building itself dates back to the early 1700s...

Ireland's only flyover pub.

CRONIN'S

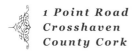

1 Point Road
Crosshaven
County Cork

THE PROVINCE OF
MUNSTER

THERE'S A BLACKBOARD BESIDE THE BAR IN CRONIN'S. IN MOST PUBS, THIS WOULD CARRY DETAILS OF TODAY'S SPECIALS OR TONIGHT'S ENTERTAINMENT. BUT NOT HERE. HERE IT'S THE TIMES OF HIGH AND LOW TIDE, THE CURRENT WATER TEMPERATURE, AND THE PHASE OF THE MOON.

Denis Cronin—could you tell he's Irish?

So, in case you were in any doubt, this is boating country. That explains all the maritime memorabilia in the pub. Though it doesn't explain all the boxing pictures, the collection of Toby Jugs in the back room, or the large brass boxing ring bell. The bell is rung every time someone puts a euro in the charity box. It rings out a lot. They're kind, friendly people around here who look out for each other and are pleased to see visitors— whether you've just arrived by road or washed up with the tide.

Sean Cronin sets the tone for the pub he's run his way for over forty years. He is a charming, affable, engaging host with a deep knowledge of many things, including whiskey. His son Denis helps out in the bar, manages the pub kitchen, and runs the very fine attached seafood restaurant, Mad Fish. In the summer, Denis will

Ahoy there—time to drop anchor and tell a tale or two about the one that got away.

often set up a street food kitchen outside, serving whatever is fresh in from the boats that morning—anything from cod to lobster.

Denis is also quite possibly the most Irish-looking man in Ireland, with curly red hair, thick red beard, and tweed waistcoat. He knows it, too, and in fact for many years he and his sister Joleen organized the international Red Head Convention here in Crosshaven.

If you were a cold, weary sailor in from the sea, we reckon this is exactly what you would imagine paradise on dry land to look like. A warm, cozy pub with a roaring fire, friendly locals, and a very generous selection of rums. Or, if you can't face another tot, how about an Irish whiskey? There are around ninety to choose from, and Sean and Denis run regular tastings to encourage sampling. There's a very impressive collection of gin, along with the trifecta of stouts: Guinness, Beamish, and Murphy's. They also take their

coffee seriously in here, which is always a good sign.

You can't really just call in to Crosshaven because you're passing: The road here only goes here. But that's OK. It's a lovely town. And Cronin's is the ideal port in any storm—even if you're an old landlubber at heart.

THE GREY HOUND

Market Square
Sleveen, Kinsale
County Cork

THE PROVINCE OF
MUNSTER

WHEN YOU'RE ONE OF THE OLDEST PUBS—
IF NOT INDEED THE OLDEST—IN IRELAND,
YOU CAN AFFORD TO SAY NO TO CHANGING
THE ODD DETAIL.

THE GREY HOUND

For Enda Burke, who has owned and run the pub with her husband since 1999, that's just the way she likes it; and so do her customers. "Change things? I wouldn't dare!" she says in all seriousness.

And that's a very good thing. Pubs like this are their own world: That's why people love them. Which is not to say that The Grey Hound is some sort of old-fashioned theme pub. Not a bit of it. It's the real thing, and has been since 1695. Yes, you read that date correctly. (What's more, the house itself is slightly older still.)

The pub is small, though there's another room upstairs and some tables outside, which are very popular in summer. (And there's actually another pub, called Holystone House, conveniently joined on in the back.) There's a red-painted snug lined with comfy benches, and open fires in winter.

Sometimes they light candles around the place in the evenings. The pub is open seven days a week, "from 11 or maybe 12 until, well, late . . ." says Enda. Make of that well-intentioned haziness what you will.

The Grey Hound—not Greyhound, mind—is named after the beloved dog of a former owner, the legendary publican Peter Barry. The place has always enjoyed a reputation for friendliness, which is fully warranted. There are no formal *seisiúns* here: The music tends to be both spontaneous and frequent. There's no food or cocktails either. There is, however, a very impressive gin selection. And this being Cork, the pub is also blessed with the holy trinity of stouts: Guinness, Murphy's, and Beamish. And amen to that.

This is very much a community pub—a place where people meet and socialize, whether it's over a drink or a coffee. Conversation in general is strongly encouraged in the Grey Hound. As Enda says, "cell phones have no place in a pub." True in 1695; true today.

*There's a
red-painted snug
lined with
comfy benches...*

*Looking well
for its age,
isn't it?*

THE SPANIARD

Scilly
Kinsale
County Cork

www.thespaniard.ie

IN 1601, DON JUAN DEL AQUILA
COMMANDED THE SPANISH ARMADA
IN SUPPORT OF THE IRISH REBELS
AGAINST THE ENGLISH IN THE BATTLE
OF KINSALE. IT DIDN'T GO SO WELL.

THE PROVINCE OF
MUNSTER

Don Juan lost the battle.
However, a few centuries later
he did get one of the Great Irish
Pubs named in his honor—which is
immortality of a far higher order.

The Spaniard is situated atop
a steepish hill overlooking the
picturesque town below. Stroll
up to it if you can: It'll make the
reward seem all the greater. The
building itself was once a small
castle or fortress. You can still see
the original seventh-century walls,
though the building feels like less
a manmade construction than a
natural wonder, as if deposited
up here long ago by a freak wave.
There's sawdust on the slanting
floor, dark wood, warm red lanterns,
and everywhere signs of the sea—
images of ships and traces of the
nautical life.

This is a small but friendly pub,
where regulars mingle easily with
visitors (and old men sit in the spot
they call Death Row!). This being

The Spaniard: well worth the schlep up the hill.

Cork, Murphy's is on tap here, as well as Beamish and Guinness. You'll also find some local craft beers and a decent whiskey selection. The Spaniard does outstanding pub food (the chowder is rightly famous), and for fine dining there's a separate restaurant building in the back.

There are regular traditional music *seisiúns* here during the week and throughout the summer. On Tuesdays there's long been a tradition of fishermen bringing in some of their daily catch, cooking it over the open fire, and sharing it out in the pub. If you're there when that happens, feel free to buy the benefactor a drink. It may be declined, but the offer is still appreciated.

So if you get the chance to visit Kinsale, pull up a rickety wicker stool at The Spaniard, drop anchor, and wait to see what happens. You never know what the tide might bring in.

THE CASTLE INN

97 South Main Street
Cork
County Cork

THE PROVINCE OF
MUNSTER

CORK'S OLDEST WORKING PUB DIVIDES
OPINION. SOME PEOPLE ADORE IT, AND
SOME PEOPLE REALLY ADORE IT. BUT,
PLEASE, DO FEEL FREE TO MAKE UP YOUR
OWN MIND.

In all seriousness, The Castle Inn isn't for everyone. For a start, it's tiny. The linoleum floor tiles are worn away. Some of the furniture is broken and the rest looks like it's about to break. The toilet facilities are both rudimentary and outside, which may well be the best place for them. There's no music, no food, and no frills.

On the other hand, what The Castle Inn does have is a fantastic snug—complete with serving window—and enough character to fill a pub ten times the size. For Michael O'Donovan, who runs the place now, it's just the family business. He was born here and grew up here. His parents still live upstairs. His mother, Mary, was a legendary character in town. "People would come in and ask specifically for her to serve them." Being thrown out by Mary was apparently also once considered something of a rite of passage for the rebellious youths of the Rebel City.

Things are a little more sedate now, but the welcome is still hearty and sincere. There's always a big open fire in winter, "which in Cork is most of the year," grins Michael. All three of the main stouts—Guinness, Murphy's, and Beamish—are available, though Michael says that Heineken is by far the biggest-selling draft. The whiskey offering is better than you might guess, with Cask Jameson, Green Spot, and several Midletons among the familiar Paddy and Powers bottles. The pub was once popular with local dockworkers and still does a brisk trade in hot rum, port, and whiskey. (No Irish Coffee, though.)

The Castle Inn is one of a dying breed, a country pub in the heart of the city. When Michael was a boy, the pub served as a community meeting place, and he recalls

often coming home from school to find a spirited discussion or raucous singsongs under way in the middle of the afternoon.

The pub has been photographed and filmed many times—because you can't artificially re-create this kind of atmosphere. You've got to seek out the real thing, and when you find it, hold on to it.

The well-trodden path to and from the bar. And back again.

THE HI-B

108 Oliver Plunkett Street
Cork
County Cork

THE PROVINCE OF
MUNSTER

THE HI-B

Rule number one in The Hi-B: no cell phones. Rule number two: See number one.

Everything about this pub is a bit eccentric, and the tone is set by its famous/infamous owner himself, Brian O'Donnell—a man for whom the Irish use of the term "a character" seems both tailor-made and yet wholly inadequate. Local legend has it that half of Cork claims to have been barred from the Hi-B by the now-retired Brian at some point. The other half actually has been.

Today, Nancy, Brian's wife, steers this quirky ship in the heart of the Rebel City. It's a true landmark, a place that inspires fierce loyalty. The pub is actually up a flight of stairs from street level (naturally, there's no elevator), which makes for an interesting bird's-eye view of the world below. It's essentially just one tiny space, furnished like a comfortable sitting room from an

The Hi-B interior: like an ordinary sitting room with some extraordinary features.

earlier era, with velvet-covered stools, heavy brocaded curtains, and comfortable stuffed armchairs. A sitting room that also happens to have a long, curved bar taking up one wall. There's an open fire, a record player, a piano. (How that made it up those stairs doesn't bear thinking about.) Sometimes the piano gets played, sometimes people put records on, and sometimes there's a guitar being strummed in a corner. And sometimes none of these things happen and people are happy talking.

There's no food here, no TV, and, in case there was really any doubt about it, no cocktails. Conversation isn't just encouraged; it's practically compulsory (hence the cell phone ban). You'll find the traditional triptych of stouts on offer here—Guinness, of course, as well as Cork's own Murphy's and Beamish—as well as some local microbrews and a decent gin selection.

You might also be wondering about the name. It was once the Hibernian Hotel, but that got shortened along the way. Someone in The Hi-B will surely tell you the whole story if you ask. And if you feel like sharing that tale with the wider world, just wait until later before you reach for your phone, OK? Because there's eccentric and then there's The Hi-B. Now, what are you having?

DE BARRA'S

55 Pearse Street
Clonakilty
County Cork

www.debarra.ie

THE PROVINCE OF
MUNSTER

NOW THIS IS A REAL TWO-FOR-ONE. BECAUSE
WITH DE BARRA'S YOU DON'T JUST GET A GENUINE
GREAT IRISH PUB BUT ALSO ONE OF THE WORLD'S
LANDMARK MUSIC HOUSES. AS CHRISTY MOORE
HIMSELF FAMOUSLY PUT IT, "THERE'S CARNEGIE
HALL, THE ROYAL ALBERT HALL, SYDNEY OPERA
HOUSE—AND THEN THERE'S DE BARRA'S."

DE BARRA'S

And the evidence is everywhere—photographs and memorabilia, instruments including fiddles, flutes, bodhráns, a saxophone, and guitars, all donated by performers and guests. There's even a bass that belonged to former longtime Clonakilty resident Noel Redding, of The Jimi Hendrix Experience. Noel played here regularly. (Look closely and you'll also find his double-platinum disc for *Are You Experienced* by the bar.)

People travel from all over for the music *seisiúns* and gigs. And even if there's nothing on, they come anyway. The fire's lit, the *craic* is ninety, as we say, and there's a pint with your name on it. As this is Cork, it's probably Murphy's or Beamish—but the other black stuff is also available, as well as some excellent local craft beers and a fine whiskey selection. There are no cocktails and none of what manager Raymond Blackburn calls "fancy food," though the soups and toasted sandwiches here are outstanding. Most of the music happens in the auditorium—a large, purpose-built back room with a stage. People sit on old school benches and around old sewing-machine tables and listen, laugh, sing, and call for more.

De Barra's is a quirky, magical place (check out the collection of masks on the wall) that Raymond himself affectionately describes as "a bit higgledy-piggledy." It just grew that way. It's been in his family for generations. Like many of the publicans we encountered when researching these bars, the Blackburns consider themselves custodians rather than owners. "We're just the keeper of the flame," says Raymond Blackburn.

Long may it continue to burn bright.

One of the world's great music venues also features an equally great bar. Win-win.

*People travel
from all
over for the
music seisiúns
and gigs . . .*

MacCARTHY'S

The Square
Castletownbere
County Cork

www.maccarthysbar.com

THE PROVINCE OF
MUNSTER

POOR ADRIENNE MACCARTHY. SHE DIDN'T
STAND A CHANCE. A NEWLY QUALIFIED
NURSE, SHE CAME OVER FROM LONDON IN
1979 TO HELP OUT WITH THE FAMILY BAR—
JUST FOR SIX MONTHS, TOPS. SHE'S STILL
HERE, AND HASN'T REGRETTED A DAY OF IT.

It's understandable. A bar like this is special. Customers off on their travels around the world send it postcards. They pine for it. Some of its stories are so extraordinary they take on a life of their own—like the tale of the samurai sword that came home from a Japanese prisoner-of-war camp after the Second World War with Adrienne's father, Doctor Aiden MacCarthy. (The extraordinary story took some seventy years to unravel, and became a book, *A Doctor's War*, and a documentary film, *A Doctor's Sword*.)

The pub itself was established in 1860, having been granted one of the first licenses in the area. It was a general store, as well, and supplied the local fishing fleets. The bar also used to serve the nearby lighthouse, and would row the provisions out in their own boat. There are stories, too, that the pub was a famous matchmaking parlor for the lovelorn. Apparently many a troth was plighted in its quiet snugs.

In the summer, there's music in MacCarthy's six nights a week. In fact, there's something going on most days, as well—the bridge club, Irish-language classes, a meeting of the local literary society, or traditional set dancing.

People travel far and near to this 2016 Irish Pub of the Year. They write books and songs and make films about it. They come for the atmosphere, the music, the company, the food (simple but sensational, especially the seafood)—and they stay. Ask Adrienne. She understands why.

The Great Irish Pub as muse: People write odes, songs, and letters home to it.

The bar also used to serve the nearby lighthouse...

J. CURRAN'S

IT WAS JAMES CURRAN'S GREAT-GREAT-GRANDFATHER WHO OPENED THIS PUB, BACK IN 1871, AND A CURRAN HAS STOOD BEHIND THE BAR EVER SINCE. MOST OF THEM HAVE ALSO BEEN CALLED JAMES, THOUGH THERE WAS ALSO A JOHN AND A JOE.

THE PROVINCE OF
MUNSTER

What does all that mean—apart from never having to repaint the "J" on the sign outside? Well, it means continuity, familiarity, character. In other words, the cornerstones of Irish pub hospitality. And that's what this pub embodies perfectly.

Curran's is still a functioning shop and pub, in the great spirit grocer tradition. The ledgers from the old days are still here, and show that almost everything was sold here at one time: coal, flour, seeds, tools, boots, meal, and cloth. The present James, great-great-grandson of the original, is something of a storyteller and happily recounts the tale from his youth of a farmer who came in to buy some supplies, including flour and coal. After a quick jar—you know, just to be sociable—he loaded them up side by side on the back of the open cart and set off. It began to rain, and by the time the farmer got home, the wet flour had become blackened from the coal. "Well, what

could he do?" says James. "He baked the black flour into bread and ate it anyway. Insisted it was best he ever tasted."

The pub is essentially one room with two counters. On one side groceries, dry goods, and clothing are sold. On the other, the goods are liquid. This is the busier of the two sides. In many ways, it's an ideal setup. For example, if you take a sudden notion for a nifty tweed cap while your pint settles, you don't have far to go. An eminently practical arrangement.

It's been said that the creamy-colored pub itself resembles the head of a well-pulled pint of Guinness. True enough. It's also said that when David Lean was here in Dingle shooting *Ryan's Daughter*, he tried to buy the pub's Guinness-black slate floor. It wasn't for sale at any price. It's still here, unchanged, like everything else.

Curran's is one of those optical illusion pubs. It's small, yet it always seems to be able to fit everyone in. There is actually a beer garden in the back, but most people

seem to stay inside, where all the *craic* is. There's endless bric-a-brac and memorabilia everywhere, ranging from a diving bell helmet in the window to a signed photograph of Robert Mitchum behind the bar. After you've been here for about an hour, that all makes perfect sense. Oh, and yes, there are snugs here: three of them, no less, where over the years many a discreet conversation was held, and often a spot of matchmaking, too. James has never seen the need to change anything. And why would he? As formulas go, this one is definitely working.

If you want to get ahead, get a hat while your pint settles.

That cream and black decor remind you of anything? Pint, please.

DICK MACK'S

47 Green Street
Dingle
County Kerry

www.dickmackspub.com

IMAGINE THE SCENARIO. LET'S SAY YOU'RE
IN A FANTASTIC OLD BAR ENJOYING THE
CRAIC AND DIVERSION WHEN SUDDENLY
YOU REALIZE, "HEY, I REALLY NEED A
NEW BELT. OH, AND A HANDMADE KEY FOB,
TOO." WHERE YOU GONNA GO? RELAX—
LUCKILY, YOU'RE IN DICK MACK'S.

*The lower painting is of the late Charles Haughey,
former taoiseach (Irish prime minister), roué,
rake, and rogue.*

As far as Irish joint enterprises
go, a pub and leatherwork shop do
admittedly make for one of the more
unusual pairings. But then Dick
Mack's is that kind of place. The
leatherwork is actually the remains of
a once-vibrant shoemaking business.
(There are still awls, lasts, and
myriad other shoemaker's tools to be
seen among the tottering towers of
shoeboxes around the place.)

Now in the hands of the fourth
Mack (MacDonnell) generation, the
pub is something of a shrine both
to eccentricity and to whiskey. In
regard to the former, just look up:
There's a currach—a traditional
Irish boat—hanging from the
ceiling. And as for the latter, there
are hundreds of whiskey bottles on
display—mostly Irish, then Scotch,
and then the rest of the world. (We
even spotted a bottle from Iceland.)
They have their own recipe maturing
at the minute, as well, along with

Owner Oliver J. MacDonnell spotted in his natural setting.

their own bottled beer from Dick Mack's Brewhouse in town.

It was 1899—long before *Ryan's Daughter*, before the arrival of Fungie the celebrity dolphin in Dingle Harbour—when this place first started serving liquid refreshments. It hasn't changed much in all that time (aside from extravagances like electricity and indoor plumbing).

The pub doesn't do food, but there is music—both frequent and spontaneous. But primarily, this is a pub for conversation, and wherever you turn your head, you'll find something new to talk about, and somebody happy to oblige. If you get a chance, ask the barman about Dolly Parton and he'll tell about the time she climbed up on the counter and made a speech, thanking the original Dick Mack for bestowing upon her the honor of a Walk of Fame star outside the door. She didn't buy any belts, though.

KENNEDY'S

Upper Main Street
Dingle
County Kerry

IF YOU'RE LOOKING FOR KENNEDY'S, IT WOULD BE HARD TO MISS. IT'S PAINTED A STRIKING CANDY-COLORED PURPLE AND GREEN COMBINATION. IF THIS WAS CONCEIVED TO CREATE WHAT REALTORS CALL "SIDEWALK APPEAL," IT'S REALLY NOT NECESSARY.

THE PROVINCE OF
MUNSTER

Michael Murphy's pub is as fantastic on the inside as it is conspicuous on the outside.

The pub belonged to his grandparents, who opened it in the 1930s and ran it until the 1970s. After they died, Michael's mother, who was working in north Kerry, would come back on the weekends just to open it up for regulars. She managed to keep this extraordinary arrangement going for years but eventually shut the pub in the 1990s. After that it stayed closed until 2014, when Michael, who had been working as a town planner in the UK, moved back and reopened the pub. Beyond freshening the paintwork and fixing whatever needed fixing, he didn't do much to it. "I wanted to keep the original character of the place as best I could," he says. "When some of the old regulars from my mother's day came in and said it hadn't changed, well, that was the greatest compliment I could have wished for."

One thing Michael did change, though, was the drinks offering. Today in Kennedy's you will of course find the requisite stouts, lagers, and spirits, but you'll also see a very impressive range of craft beers and ciders—around ten on draft and another thirty in bottles. For the most part, these are local Irish products, such as West Kerry Beer and Black's of Kinsale. These were selected partly from a desire to support local business and partly because the quality is so high. "These beers and ciders are flying here—and if they weren't really good, customers would let us know quickly enough!" Michael adds.

The pub is tiny but bright and airy. There is a small snug and, outside, an old cowshed and courtyard that Michael intends to develop at some point—but there's no rush. There's some memorabilia round the walls in Kennedy's and on shelves and nooks, but not an overpowering amount. One key piece is a vast steamer trunk that serves as a table in the back room. It belonged to his grandmother and went with her when she emigrated to the States as a young girl. Eventually it made the long crossing back to Kerry and here—a fitting journey's end.

One key piece
is a vast
steamer trunk
that serves as
a table . . .

The snug in Kennedy's is, well, snug.

Grandmother's steamer trunk:
home at last.

O'LOCHLAINN'S

Ballyvaughan
County Clare

THE PROVINCE OF
MUNSTER

"THINGS ARE FLUID IN IRELAND," SAYS MARGARET O'LOCHLAINN, SOMEWHAT STATING THE OBVIOUS. SHE'S TALKING ABOUT HER RELAXED APPROACH TO OPENING HOURS, BUT SHE COULD JUST AS EASILY BE REFERRING TO WHAT HAPPENS INSIDE THE EXTRAORDINARY PUB THAT'S BEEN IN HER FAMILY FOR SIX GENERATIONS (WITH ANOTHER GENERATION WAITING IN THE WINGS).

For O'Lochlainn's is a strange natural phenomenon—like those mysterious roads where the cars roll uphill or lakes that vanish and reappear overnight. Here, in this tiny pub in a tiny village on the edge of the beautiful, mystical landscape of the Burren, time simply gets lost. You step in for a quick one and when you look around, the entire evening has sped by. So you come back tomorrow, and it's the same mystifying story all over again.

What happens is that Margaret will greet you as though she's been waiting for you all this time. And before you know it, she'll serve you the perfect pint, then the perfect whiskey. And with that, a thought will form in your mind: "I'm going to stay here; I never want to leave." This is empirically proven scientific fact. Don't even bother trying to question it. Maybe you'll be dazzled by the collection of some five hundred whiskeys. Maybe you'll even sample a couple of the seventy-odd that Margaret has for sale. Or it could be the endless conversation that's been going back and forth across the bar and looping around the room for year upon year upon year that catches you. Or maybe it's the music session over there that's just materialized out of thin air while you were looking out the window at Galway Bay.

And maybe, like other natural mysteries, this one is best left unexplained. That way you get to savor it afresh again and again.

A word of caution, though. If you're in a hurry, you're in the wrong place. So relax. Tomorrow will take care of itself. It always does, especially when you understand that, deep down, the important things really are fluid.

"Ah, there you are." Margaret makes even strangers feel she's been expecting them all this time.

AND WHILE YOU'RE IN MUNSTER . . .

As a rule, things in Ireland are designed for comfort, not for speed. We like to take our time to enjoy the surroundings, the company, the *craic*; and of course we recommend you do the same. Munster offers a great deal to discover—more than we can fit into these pages. But we couldn't leave the province without mentioning these extra must-see places.

FOYNES FLYING BOAT & MARITIME MUSEUM

Main Street, Foynes, Co. Limerick
www.flyingboatmuseum.com

The small, picturesque town of Foynes on the banks of the Shannon, Ireland's longest river, has played a remarkable role in the history of transatlantic flight, of Ireland's maritime trade, of the creation of famous drinks, and even of the U.S. Civil War.

*Ireland's best Irish Coffee is made right here, wher
it was invented.*

The museum is home to the world's only full-size replica of a Boeing 314 Clipper, the luxurious flying boats that brought the rich and famous from the United States across the Atlantic in the 1930s and 1940s. Here you will also find the Irish Coffee Lounge. For it was in this place that in 1943 one of the world's most famous drinks was invented, by chef Joe Sheridan. The whole story is re-created in the lounge—and of course you get to sample Joe's wondrous creation. (By our reckoning, the best in Ireland.)

The separate maritime museum presents many facets of life and trade on the Shannon, with exhibits on the types of ships that used the river, from traditional Irish currachs to paddle steamers. And that Civil War reference? There's a display of Confederate uniforms, which were actually manufactured in Limerick and shipped out of Ireland—through Foynes.

KNAPPOGUE CASTLE

Quin Road, Ennis, Co. Clare

www.shannonheritage.com

Knappogue Castle is a beautifully restored medieval tower house dating back as far as the fifteenth century. Within the grounds there is a walled garden and a separate rose garden. The castle isn't open to the public but is available for private group bookings. Between April and October there is a regular evening medieval banquet, complete with costumes, music, and feasting. Anyone can go to this, but reservations are required.

Knappogue Castle is today maintained and run by Shannon Heritage. However, the original restoration work was begun in the late 1960s by Texan Mark Andrews, who bought the castle with his wife, Lavonne, a noted architect. Mark accumulated a large private whiskey collection, including one he called Knappogue Castle. His son later commercially launched the whiskey under the same name.

There's whiskey in the bar. Lots of it.

CELTIC WHISKEY BAR & LARDER

Incorporating the Irish Whiskey Experience

93 New Street, Killarney, Co. Kerry

www.celticwhiskeybar.com
www.irishwhiskeyexperience.net

Is it a pub, a high-end cocktail bar, a fine restaurant, a shrine to all things *uisce beatha*? Answer: yes, yes, yes, and most definitely yes.

The brainchild of Ally Alpine, founder of the celebrated Celtic Whiskey Shop & Wines on the Green in Dublin, The Celtic Whiskey Bar & Larder is the home of Ireland's largest whiskey collection—upwards of 1,400 bottles, of which over 800 are Irish. And, what's even more special about the collection is that the whiskeys are all for sale by the measure. You can expect to see—and taste—some rarities, obscure bottlings, as well as some very special Irish whiskeys produced exclusively for the Larder.

And of course, there's more. The Irish Whiskey Experience is effectively an extension of the Larder. It is described as "a sensory and interactive experience," guiding novices and experts alike with tours, tastings, and classes on everything from food pairing and cocktails to cask finishing and blending your own Irish whiskey.

THE PROVINCE OF
CONNACHT

THE COUNTIES OF
CONNACHT

Galway
Leitrim
Mayo
Roscommon
Sligo

VISITING
CONNACHT

WELCOME TO THE WEST! AND YES, IT IS WILD OUT HERE IN IRELAND'S
LEAST POPULOUS PROVINCE. CONNACHT COMPRISES FIVE COUNTIES:
GALWAY, LEITRIM, MAYO, ROSCOMMON, AND SLIGO. TO COMPLICATE
MATTERS A LITTLE, SOME OF THIS IS ALSO CONNEMARA, WHICH IS NEITHER
A PROVINCE NOR A COUNTY BUT SOMEWHERE BETWEEN A GEOGRAPHIC
DISTRICT AND A FRAME OF MIND. IN A COUNTRY OF SPECTACULAR SCENERY,
HERE IS WHERE WE KEEP SOME OF THE BEST STUFF.

W hat's more, Ireland isn't a
large country, yet it's surprisingly
easy to discover places that look
wholly untouched by human
presence. For example, Doolough
Pass in Mayo. There's a valley
and a lake and a road. And you.
That's it. Or the Connemara Lakes
themselves: water, heather, silence,
and maybe the odd trout taking a
leap. In Galway, take the Sky Road
down to the lovely town of Clifden.
It's one of the most magnificent
coastal routes in the country
(and we've quite a few of those).
Galway city itself is a buzzing, arty,
bohemian outpost right on the edge
of the Atlantic. It's an ancient place,
but—dare we say it—like a great
whiskey, it has aged well. You'll like
it there.

In certain ways, Connacht is
old Ireland. It has kept many
of the traditions and, of course,
the language. The West Galway

*Dún Briste (The Broken Fort)—an impressive sea stack
just off Downpatrick Head, County Mayo.*

All unchanged, unchanged utterly: the timeless beauty of Yeats Country.

Gaeltacht (Irish-speaking region) is the largest in Ireland, with tens of thousands of native speakers who use the language every day. If you do encounter some, don't worry. Everyone speaks English, too.

Sligo is often referred to as Yeats Country. It is where our great poet grew up, the place W.B. returned to time and again, and where he is buried. You can visit the inspiration of one of his most famous poems, "The Lake Isle of Innisfree," among many other notable places on the well-signposted Yeats circuit.

Now, although Connacht may be old Ireland, it's most certainly not old-fashioned. Looking for some golf, diving, a yoga retreat? Or how about a gallery, a chic restaurant, an even chicer nightclub? We've got all those. Then of course there's the pubs. Ah, the pubs. That's where a lot of the music and *craic* lives, and you wouldn't want to miss any of that now, would you?

Killary Harbour, Ireland's only fjord, forms the border between Counties Galway and Mayo. Beautiful, isn't it?

A SHORT HISTORY OF DISTILLING IN CONNACHT

"To Hell or to Connaught!" was the rock-and-a-hard-place choice reportedly given by English military commander and eternal bête noire Oliver Cromwell to the native Irish in 1653 during the Plantation. This mass clearance saw English settlers handed the good, rich land in the East and the Irish banished to the inhospitable West—or to an even worse fate.

Though the full history of that account is more nuanced, what's not in doubt is the nature of the landscape of Connaught (or Connacht) awaiting the Irish out here in internal exile. With its poor, stony soil and harsh climate, Connacht was definitely a challenge. Yet people found a way to subsist there, as they always have, eking out a living from the land and the sea. And of course, making whiskey or, more accurately, *poitín*—Irish moonshine. In this particular regard, the region had one great advantage: Its inaccessibility made detection from the Crown's tax inspectors difficult. Predictably, illegal distilling prospered here. However, so too did the legal trade. By the eighteenth century there were several official, licensed distilleries, and Galway city itself had become a thriving port with a rich reputation in the wine trade.

A particular style of whiskey developed out here in the West—in general smokier, more peaty, and perhaps a little less refined than the spirit the great Dublin distilleries were producing in their heyday. After all, just like a fine wine, whiskey has terroir.

When the Irish industry began to collapse in the late nineteenth century, distilling in Connacht all but vanished. Even *poitín*-making eventually declined. But today it is back after more than a hundred years, in robust health and filled with energy, passion, and purpose.

For example, in The Shed Distillery in Drumshanbo, County Leitrim, innovation and experimentation are the very DNA of the place, and these combine with a deep respect for tradition. In Connacht Distillery in County Mayo, two great traditions—the Irish and the American—are being fused and producing exciting new products, while giving old ones an inspired twist.

If you head out west along the spectacular Wild Atlantic Way and stop to watch the waves racing to the shore, be sure also to make the time to discover a little of the unique story of distilling in Connacht. And remind yourself that Cromwell got it wrong. For this is not Hell. Quite the opposite.

CONNACHT
DISTILLERIES
OF TODAY

*In The Shed a still lets off steam
after another extraordinary day.*

CONNACHT DISTILLERY

THERE WAS NO EUREKA MOMENT. THIS WAS A STORY
OF EVOLUTION, OF AN IDEA THAT WAS SLOWLY
TAKING SHAPE IN THE MINDS OF SEVERAL PEOPLE
INDEPENDENTLY AT THE SAME TIME—WITH AN OCEAN
BETWEEN THEM.

Belleek
Ballina
County Mayo

www.connachtwhiskey.com

THE PROVINCE OF
CONNACHT

— *A transatlantic family affair, bottled.*

It turned out they all harbored a dream of bringing back single malt pot still Irish whiskey to the west of Ireland, from where it had effectively disappeared over a century ago.

P.J. Stapleton, a successful attorney living in Philadelphia, was visiting his Irish cousin, David Stapleton, a manufacturing engineer from County Galway. On the links of Connemara Golf Club, they walked and talked, and eventually the conversation turned to whiskey; and more specifically, the dearth of craft Irish distilleries.

P.J., who was a past chairman of both the Pennsylvania Liquor Control Board and the National Alcohol Beverage Control Board, was of a mind that America needed more choice in Irish whiskey. David wanted to provide that choice.

Suddenly a happenstance conversation was shaping into an idea to build a craft whiskey distillery in the west of Ireland. Could it be done? With the right partners and expertise on board, they thought that maybe it could. The plan was beginning to take shape.

Enter Tom Jensen, a friend of P.J.'s and a U.S. drinks industry veteran who had founded a craft whiskey distillery in Philadelphia. Award-winning master distiller Robert Cassell, also from Philadelphia but with local Irish roots, came on board at this stage, too. Next task: Find a location.

The huge old bakery building on the banks of the River Moy in County Mayo had been derelict for twenty-five years. It was just a shell, but it was, says David, perfect: a rough diamond. In keeping with the company's ethos, the new handmade fittings were commissioned from local craftspeople and artisans. That care is evident everywhere, from the copper pot stills designed by the master distiller to the metalwork on the walkways and in the fitting out and finishing of the visitor center.

David Stapleton sets them up.

The distillery uses local water from the River Ox and Loughs Conn and Cullin. The maritime climate in the west of Ireland is not conducive to growing barley, so they carefully select their Irish-grown grain according to a bespoke mashbill, and dry mill their own malt at the distillery. Bottling is a manual affair, as are most processes here.

Connacht considers itself a family distiller that intends to remain a small-batch, high-quality craft producer, not a spirits factory. The company's goal is to continue to produce limited-quantity, premium Irish whiskey, gin, vodka, and *poitín* that are very much influenced by their place of origin, or terroir. The founders believe that the climatic conditions of the location—given its proximity to the river and loughs, and with the wild Atlantic Ocean just a couple of kilometers away—are a contributing factor in the flavor of the spirits. And they've been right so far.

This is a company that was born out of a conversation and an idea. It is also a family company with feet in two continents. The Irish and the American sides are equal here, each mindful and respectful of the other. The history of how the family lines developed separately forms part of the distillery itself, and is represented on the labels by the figure of a dragon, once the symbol of terra incognita for all those voyaging into the unknown. The future here is less uncertain. But the sense of adventure endures.

Local craftspeople designed and built the metalwork around Robert Cassell's handsome stills.

Checking the distillate. Yip, another good one.

AT A GLANCE

FIRST DISTILLATION
2015

STILLS
3 Pot Stills (Wash Still 2,500L, Intermediate Still 1,800L, Spirit Still 1,400L)

LPA
130,000

WHISKEY STYLES
Single Malt & Pot Still

VISITOR CENTER/TOURS
Yes

KEY BOTTLINGS

CONNACHT IRISH WHISKEY
ABV: 43%

BROTHERSHIP IRISH-AMERICAN BLENDED WHISKEY
ABV: 45%

SPADE & BUSHEL CASK STRENGTH 10-YEAR-OLD SINGLE MALT IRISH WHISKEY
ABV: 57.5%

BALLYHOO GRAIN IRISH WHISKEY
ABV: 43%

THE SHED DISTILLERY

IT'S RIGHT THERE ON THE SIGN AT THE DOOR: "FIRST DISTILLERY IN CONNACHT IN 101 YEARS." THEY'RE PROUD OF THAT, AND RIGHTLY SO. WITH ITS GLEAMING COPPER STILLS AND DECIDEDLY HANDS-ON ETHOS, THE SHED PROMISES A RETURN TO TRADITIONAL METHODS OF SPIRIT-MAKING IN A WILD CORNER OF RURAL IRELAND.

Carrick-on-Shannon Road
Drumshanbo
County Leitrim

www.thesheddistillery.com

THE PROVINCE OF
CONNACHT

B ut that doesn't mean that this unique, multipurpose distillery is in thrall to the past. Far from it, because innovation rules here, as well. And there's a simple explanation for this apparent contradiction: founder P.J. Rigney.

P.J. is the quintessential maverick hiding in plain view. He has spent a lifetime in the drinks business, with spells at Grants and Gilbeys— including ten years managing Baileys in international markets. Along the way he has created several successful brands, including Brian Boru Vodka, Sheridan Irish Cream, and Clontarf Irish Whiskey.

But beneath that successful, corporate exterior there was a pioneering, risk-taking spirit simply biding its time. That time came in 2014, when P.J. opened The Shed in what had been a derelict former jam factory in the village of Drumshanbo on the shores of Lough Allen in County Leitrim. He'd been looking for the right

Laid down and stacking up: The Shed's stock is building.

location for some time but immediately knew this was the one. (P.J. admits there may also have been a little divine intervention involved: His parents met here in the town seventy years earlier.)

The beginnings of the distillery were modest but always ambitious. Three state-of-the-art German copper stills were commissioned for the production of what P.J. refers to as "the premier grand cru: triple-distilled single malt Irish whiskey." A column still for gin was also installed, which was soon put to very good use.

The Shed uses no source whiskey. Its own stock is still maturing—mainly single pot still and some single malt. But the indications are very promising, as the new-make was some of the very best we sampled while compiling this book.

The majority of the first casks distilled in 2014 were snapped up by investors and collectors, including Prince Albert of Monaco and Count Carl Graf von Hardenberg of the German drinks dynasty. In the meantime, however, P.J. and head distiller Brian Taft, formerly of Dingle Whiskey Distillery, were thinking about gin: super premium Irish gin with, naturally, a difference.

Drumshanbo Gunpowder Irish Gin is made with a range of unusual and exotic herbaceous Chinese botanicals—and, distinctively, gunpowder tea—along with local Irish botanicals and fresh fruit. The product became a huge success very quickly, winning awards and finding enthusiastic new markets across the world.

The label of Drumshanbo Gin also carries a message, "From the curious mind of P.J. Rigney," and curiosity does abound here. In the works are a liqueur made from meadowsweet, a local wild plant; and another called My Three Graces, which is a Blackforest Gateau cream liqueur. In 2017 The Shed launched Sausage Tree Vodka, which combines extracts of the African kigelia fruit and Irish nettles. Before that, it created Von Hallers Gin, featuring handpicked aromatic plants and German ginger from the famous botanical gardens in Göttingen. The Shed's new visitor center will feature a greenhouse where the flora for new and future experiments will be cultivated.

But what about the whiskey, you ask. The setup is very impressive, with six fermenters, a mash tun, two mills, and two grain silos on-site. Aging is done in bourbon casks, although, predictably, there

An inspired use of copper: The Shed's gleaming stills.

The ever-curious P.J. Rigney.

AT A GLANCE

FIRST DISTILLATION
2014

STILLS
4 Hybrid Stills

LPA

WHISKEY STYLES
Single Malt & Pot Still

VISITOR CENTER/TOURS
Yes

KEY BOTTLINGS

DRUMSHANBO SINGLE POT STILL IRISH WHISKEY

are plans to experiment—with sherry casks, as well as ex-Burgundy, pinot noir, Bordeaux, and Marsala barrels. Chill filtering is carried out in-house. P.J. and Brian are also working on expressions with organic oats, rye, and wheat. The long-term goal is simple: to produce the finest single pot still Irish whiskey. And already the signs are auspicious. The Shed has the vision of P.J. Rigney and the superior technical know-how of head distiller Brian Taft. It also has a passionate, committed, and enthusiastic team on board. It has the location and the equipment. This all looks like less of a grand experiment and more of a copper-bottomed sure thing.

CONNACHT'S GREAT IRISH PUBS

*Sometimes the definition of
eclectic gets stretched to the
breaking point.*

GARAVAN'S

46 William Street
Galway
County Galway

www.garavans.ie

THE PROVINCE OF
CONNACHT

IF IT'S WHISKEY YOU'RE AFTER, INTREPID TRAVELER, GO WEST UNTO THE HEART OF LOVELY, LIVELY GALWAY CITY. THAT'S WHERE YOU'LL FIND THE OVERALL IRISH WHISKEY BAR OF THE YEAR 2017 AND THE CONNACHT WHISKEY BAR OF THE YEAR 2014, 2015, 2016, 2017 . . . AS YOU MAY SURMISE, A THEME IS STARTING TO EMERGE.

But first, a little background. Garavan's is more than a pub. It's a landmark. The building itself dates back to around 1650 and is a protected property (or listed, as it's called in Ireland). Mercifully, this restricts the possibilities for structural change. While parts of the building are old, most of it is very old, possibly even medieval. All of it is remarkable.

Before Charlie Garavan opened his pub here in 1937, this was a general merchant and wholesaler. It then became a spirit grocer. In fact, you can still see many of the old ledger accounts on display. (Ask nicely for a look: They make for pretty entertaining reading.)

Something else you'll see on display of course is a lot of *uisce beatha*. At present, the collection stands at around 170 bottles, of which some 140-odd are Irish. For the connoisseur, this means a chance to get up close and personal with some real rarities and beauties. And for

the interested beginner, Garavan's offers a range of whiskey flights or sampling platters to give your palate an idea of what it's been missing all these years.

There are also regular tastings and whiskey-themed events here—the brainchild of the current owner/resident fanatic. Paul Garavan grew up here in the family business. Whiskey is his passion, but the pub is his obsession. He knows it in every detail, quite possibly down to the atomic level. He will always strive to preserve the traditional heart of the pub but present it in a modern light. So this is no museum piece: It's the real deal, filled every night with faithful regulars who come for the music, the superlative pints, the atmosphere, and, yes, the *craic*. They don't come for the food, because there is none. But other, greater sustenance is offered.

Those regulars also come to see familiar faces, on both sides of the bar. Many of Garavan's staff have been here through generations of owners, and of customers. One of them, Tommy Kelly, spent his entire working life here, and became something of an attraction in himself for

A passion for whiskey pervades Garavan's.

his erudition and opinions, notably on Shakespeare, Dickens, opera, and, well, everything. In fact, a local journalist began writing a weekly column based on Tommy's good-natured pontifications. They've since been collected into book form, *Days and Nights in Garavan's*, which you can purchase in the bar.

Garavan's is an orderly, tidy pub with a minimum of memorabilia and bric-a-brac about the walls. Doubtless that's a deliberate strategy to encourage you to concentrate on the business at hand, which is conviviality and hospitality at their finest.

One last thing. Ghosts. Of course there are a few, but they're friendly folk who are just happy to be here. Which is perfectly, supernaturally understandable.

O'CONNOR'S FAMOUS PUB

Salthill House, Upper Salthill
Galway
County Galway

www.oconnorsbar.com

SOMETIMES LANGUAGE JUST RUNS OUT OF ROAD. IT TAKES
A LONG LOOK, SHRUGS ITS LOVELY SHOULDERS, AND SAYS,
"PASS." SURE, IT MIGHT BE TEMPTING TO DIG DEEP, TRY A
FEW HAIL MARYS—A HODGEPODGE, A MISHMASH, A FARRAGO,
MAYBE EVEN A GALLIMAUFRY OR A SALMAGUNDI—BUT IN THE
END, LANGUAGE KNOWS WHEN IT'S BEATEN.

THE PROVINCE OF
CONNACHT

O'CONNOR'S FAMOUS PUB

And it's well and truly defeated here, in the face of O'Connor's Famous Pub.

Well, just try to take this all in. The almost life-sized statue of John Wayne from *The Quiet Man*. The clothes drying on a line across the open fire. The clocks and crocks. The pots and road signs. The mirrors and bells and lanterns. The pictures of the Sacred Heart and the statues of the Child of Prague. The photographs and newspaper clippings. The candles and animal heads. The wagon wheel, the ship's wheels, the propeller. The netted constellation of seashells overhead.

Oh my. We're definitely through the looking glass now and straight into Wonderland via Salthill. And yet the decor is not the only interesting thing about O'Connor's. This is undeniably a destination pub, a must-see stop on the tourist trails. But it's no theme bar. It just happens to have been run by three generations of a family of eccentrics since it first opened in 1942.

They never really bought in to the idea of minimalism in O'Connor's Famous Pub.

Tom O'Connor, grandson of the original owner (also Thomas), tempers his natural eccentricity with a flair for understatement. "It's pretty unique," he'll admit. He runs the pub these days with his brother Frank and fully appreciates the responsibility that comes with owning a landmark. O'Connor's has, of course, been featured in many films, videos, and photo shoots, and has attracted many celebrity visitors. But no one outshines this place. It's bigger than the lot of them.

O'Connor's is a traditional Irish singing pub, with live music almost every night. The Guinness is famously good in a famously demanding town. There's an impressive collection of some forty Irish whiskeys behind the bar, and about the same number of gins.

Unusually, the pub only opens in the evening. There's no food, no TV, no piped music here. Then again, you'll never be stuck for something to talk about. Just look up. Or around, or behind, or . . . well, you get the picture. The words will follow, eventually.

GAYNOR'S

Leenane
County Galway

THE PROVINCE OF
CONNACHT

YOU MAY RECOGNIZE THE INTERIOR OF THIS PUB—
ESPECIALLY IF YOU'VE SEEN *THE FIELD*, THE ICONIC AND
HEARTRENDING FILM FROM 1990 STARRING RICHARD
HARRIS, JOHN HURT, BRENDA FRICKER, AND TOM
BERENGER. (IT WAS BASED ON THE NOVEL OF THE SAME
NAME BY THE DISTINGUISHED LATE IRISH WRITER JOHN
B. KEANE—HIMSELF ONCE THE OWNER OF A VERY FINE
PUB IN LISTOWEL, COUNTY KERRY.)

GAYNOR'S

Much of the movie was shot on location here in Leenane, and the pub was featured prominently. In fact, it was more than that. This pub was, in a sense, created for the movie. Gaynor's had of course already been here for a long time—since the nineteenth century in fact, but the filmmakers built an authentic new interior right on top of the existing one. It's still there. And there's a good reason for that: Irish resourcefulness. *The Field* has become a bit of a cottage industry around here, a stopping point along the breathtaking Wild Atlantic Way. People come from all over to find out about where the film was made. And in Gaynor's they find an honest, authentic Irish pub that's big on welcome and hospitality.

But there's more to the place than a brush with Hollywood. For a start, it's always been in the family. Generations of Gaynors have lived and worked here. Understandably, then, the pub feels like home, with an indefinable yet unmistakable warmth and familiarity that's evident as soon as you step inside.

And like home, people miss it. In fact, they send it presents from all over the world—specifically, yet inexplicably, hats. Breda Gaynor, who is the great-granddaughter of the original owner, now runs the pub, and she hangs a changing selection over the bar. She has plenty to choose from, around three hundred to date.

In terms of drinks, Gaynor's serves a very fine pint of Guinness, and is also one of the few pubs outside County Cork where you'll find Beamish on tap. There is a fair whiskey and spirits selection, a decent wine list, plus a number of bottled real ales.

They've always done very good pub grub here—soup, toasted sandwiches, chowder, and stew, etc.—but Breda recently installed a full commercial kitchen, so the food offering is going to broaden significantly. As for the drinks, they'll probably stay the same. Well, there are some things that even Hollywood can't improve.

Forget Tinseltown: This is true glamour, Galway style.

Generations of Gaynors have lived and worked here...

SHOOT THE CROWS

FIRST OF ALL, THE NAME. WE'VE GOT TO DISCUSS THAT. WELL, IN THE EARLY PART OF THE LAST CENTURY CROWS WERE CONSIDERED RURAL PESTS. THEY STOLE SEED AND CAUSED HAVOC WITH CROPS. TO CUT A LONG AND SORRY STORY SHORT, THEY HAD TO GO.

THE PROVINCE OF
CONNACHT

And so there was a bounty placed upon them. This was paid once a week in town, on production of the grim evidence. However, this didn't always suit the busy schedules of the local avian assassins, who might be otherwise engaged on that day. Enter an enterprising Sligo publican, who decided he'd accept the birds in lieu of payment in his pub, and exchange them later himself for the cash. He would then gather up all the birds, lash them to his bike, and wobble off in a cloud of feathers to the payment office in order to claim his reward.

In due course, therefore, the pub became known locally as Shoot The Crows. And believe it or not, the name is the least remarkable thing about this place. Many of the pubs featured in this book celebrate a particular aspect of Irishness—its sporting history, for example, or its literary or musical culture. This is the only one where mythology is the thing. Scenes, characters, symbols

Ronan's pub is full of character, myth, and stories but almost entirely devoid of right angles.

are everywhere here, even painted onto the windows. In fact, the entire tiny space is filled with strange artifacts and local artworks. Oh yes, and the place sort of leans over to one side, as well, but just a bit.

It's hardly surprising. Though there's been a pub here since 1876—impressive enough, you might say—the building itself dates back much further, to the late seventeenth century. A few years ago when they had to excavate part of the floor, they found a cannonball dating back to the Jacobite wars. So a little bit of slant is nothing to get too excited about.

There's music here four nights a week, with everything from traditional Irish to gypsy jazz, rock, and bluegrass. Lots of musicians live in this part of Ireland, and Shoot The Crows is something of a magnet, a fine place either to ply your trade or to appreciate that of others.

And while you're doing so, enjoy an exceptionally fine pint, or peruse the impressive whiskey selection. Other spirits are available, by the way, including numerous gins and some craft beers.

Everything about Shoot's—as it's familiarly known—says "Welcome." The seats are just right. The light is just right. The decor is just right. It's warm and a bit worn around the edges—lived in, you might say—and none the worse for that. It is what it is: You can't fight this.

Though he's had his name over the door since 1991, Ronan Watters is one of that special breed who think of themselves as custodians or stewards rather than pub owners. Shoot The Crows has been here for nearly 150 years, he says, and if he has anything to do with it, it'll be here for another 150. Well, it's got the great heroes of Irish legend looking over the place, hasn't it? We reckon it's in safe hands.

McLYNN'S

Old Market Street
Abbeyquarter North
Sligo
County Sligo

SOMETHING VERY INTERESTING HAPPENED IN 1899. MARCONI SUCCESSFULLY TRANSMITTED A SIGNAL ACROSS THE ENGLISH CHANNEL. NOW, REPORTS DO VARY, BUT IT'S ENTIRELY POSSIBLE THAT THE SIGNAL SAID, "GET TO SLIGO. McLYNN'S IS OPEN."

THE PROVINCE OF
CONNACHT

Since that momentous event, the pub has been in the hands of just one family. It had been run for many years by Alfie McLynn when one day, out of the blue, he handed his keys to his son Donal and said, "It's yours." He then ambled off for a drink—in another pub down the street. He was a contrarian, Alfie.

Donal was a newly qualified teacher at the time, with a blossoming parallel career in the family folk group. Then he had a bright idea. Instead of traveling the length and breadth of Ireland, he'd gig in his own pub. And lo, the people did come from far and wide, night after night.

McLynn's quickly acquired a reputation as a singing pub. Donal (universally known as The Dude) would keep things going, manage the bar all evening, and then get up in the morning for a full day's teaching. He's retired now, but somewhat unsuccessfully, so he's still likely to turn up and maybe even give a song or two.

In the meantime, this wonderful pub is now run by his son, Dara, a man who clearly loves his work as much as his workplace. "Well, you couldn't do it if you didn't love it, could you?" he says, with modesty. He knows the story of every photo, every knickknack, every piece of memorabilia; and that's a lot of stories.

Now certainly there are older pubs and there are grander pubs. There are pubs with greater literary or architectural heritage. But we're pretty sure there are none more comfortable, because McLynn's manages to do that thing only truly special pubs can do: They make you feel as if you've been coming here all your life, even if it's your first time. The place is instantly, immediately familiar somehow.

McLynn's has a fully justified reputation for a fine pint, and has a good whiskey selection, including some rarities on display. But the attraction isn't any one thing. It's all of the above, stirred up and served next to a roaring open fire.

That's what your man Marconi was on about, probably.

*They make you feel
you've been coming
here all your life . . .*

Make yourself comfortable—there'll be a song along in a minute.

THOMAS CONNOLLY'S

Markievicz Road and Holborn Street
Sligo
County Sligo

www.thomasconnollysligo.com

ONE OF THE FIRST THINGS YOU NOTICE ABOUT
THIS PUB IS THAT THERE ARE A LOT OF CLOCKS
AROUND THE PLACE. WHEREVER YOU TURN YOUR
HEAD, IT SEEMS, YOU CAN CHECK THE TIME,
SHOULD YOU REALLY WANT TO.

THE PROVINCE OF
CONNACHT

THOMAS CONNOLLY'S

You see, this is a place where tempus most definitely does fugit. Time becomes elastic and sort of, well, vague. The next thing you know, it's tomorrow already. Perhaps the clocks are just a sort of metaphysical Connolly joke.

There's been a licensed public house on this spot since 1861. There was probably an unlicensed one—or shebeen—here long before that. The place has got booze in its bones. The name Thomas Connolly first appeared over the door in 1890, the same year that the publican got himself elected mayor of Sligo. He'd made his fortune in America on the railroads and did what so few Irish emigrants managed to do: He came back. He then got involved in nationalist politics and even managed to persuade Ireland's uncrowned king, Charles Stewart Parnell, to visit the pub. (This was, of course, before Parnell's fall from grace in a divorce scandal. O tempora, o mores.)

Four generations of the same family have stood behind this bar, and that continuity is part of what gives Thomas Connolly's its special quality. True, there is a certain olde-worlde air about the place, with its dark, aged wood worn smooth with the years, its array of antique drawers, and vintage grocery paraphernalia (actually in use up until the 1980s). The snugs and partitions along the bar have a slightly ecclesiastical look about them, with their little steeples at the top. The staff are famously courteous, too.

However, this is no museum piece. Thomas Connolly's is a resolutely modern pub that happens to be wearing vintage clothes. There is a TV (though only for showing sports); frequent—and fantastic—live music; and a markedly progressive attitude toward the drinks, as well. This pub is proudly part of the official Irish Whiskey Trail and offers some eighty-plus bottles of Irish, Scotch, and bourbon, along with regular tastings and events. There is even a rotating craft beer lineup. However, Guinness, of course, is still the pint of choice here, and a superlative one it is, too.

Time just seems to get lost in here, we're happy to relate.

Thomas Connolly's is run these days by Paul O'Donnell, a direct descendant of the old mayor. He introduced the craft beers, and he's equally evangelical about the whiskey collection, which does contain some Irish rarities from Midleton and Bushmills. In a sense, that passion is just another aspect of the tradition that is so much part of the place. As was the case with many public houses, Thomas Connolly's used to bottle its own whiskey. The spirit would arrive in great jars and the publican would determine the strength at which it was bottled. All of the old equipment—the brass hydrometer and scales, etc.—is still there on view, along with old ledgers from the grocery days.

Thomas Connolly's isn't a huge pub, but it has many nooks and alcoves that make it feel bigger than it is. It seems like there's always another corner to discover. That's part of its charm; even its magic. Because while you're here, you can't imagine being anywhere else. It feels like exactly where you're supposed to be.

There's one more thing. The big clock, the one behind the bar? It's older than the pub itself. Now that's got to be the best joke of the lot.

THE PROVINCE OF
ULSTER

THE COUNTIES OF
ULSTER

Antrim   *Down*
Armagh   *Fermanagh*
Cavan   *Monaghan*
Derry   *Tyrone*
Donegal

VISITING ULSTER

REPUTATIONS ARE LIKE OIL TANKERS: THEY'RE HARD TO TURN AROUND. BUT BELFAST HAS MANAGED IT, AND DONE SO IN QUITE SOME STYLE. THESE DAYS THE FIRST CITY OF IRELAND'S NORTHERN PROVINCE IS A PLACE TRANSFORMED, WITH GREAT VISITOR ATTRACTIONS, EXCELLENT RESTAURANTS AND NIGHTLIFE, AND FANTASTIC SHOPPING. IN SHORT, IT HAS EVERYTHING A MODERN CAPITAL SHOULD HAVE.

The fact that we do have these things is still slightly surprising to those of us who grew up here in the dark days. But we did it. We turned the tanker round.

People are coming, and so are the accolades. In the last year or so *National Geographic*, *Lonely Planet*, and *Condé Nast Traveler* have all given Belfast a big thumbs-up. In 2016 Titanic Belfast was named the world's leading tourist attraction. But there's a lot more to see here in addition to the substantial Titanic industry. (And before you say anything about the ship, just remember—it was fine when it left here.)

If you're heading north from Belfast, do yourself a favor and take the Causeway Coastal Route. It goes all the way to the famous Giant's Causeway itself, and is one of the most picturesque drives you'll ever experience, taking in no fewer than three officially designated Areas of Outstanding Natural Beauty.

The hauntingly romantic ruins of Dunluce Castle.

Ireland's tallest cliffs— Sliabh Liag on the wild Donegal coast.

Catch your breath, then make for Derry, and take a tour of its famous medieval walls.

If stately homes, museums, and castles are your thing, we pack a surprising number of them into a very small space. Then again, we've also managed to find room for over ninety golf courses, including a couple of the best in the world—Royal County Down and Royal Portrush.

We've arranged a lot of scenery for you, too, from the silent wilderness of the Sperrin Mountains to the majestic sweep of the Mournes, from the beautiful beaches of Donegal to the exquisite Fermanagh Lakelands.

Northern Ireland has become something of a foodie destination, as well, with many artisan products, outstanding meat and seafood, craft beers and spirits, dairy products, and more. You may need to loosen your belt a notch or two.

Another phenomenon that's emerged in recent years is a *Game of Thrones* tourism industry. It's huge. The show is partially filmed in Northern Ireland, so if you've got the time, yes, we've got the dragons . . .

The Giant's Causeway: Every stone is hexagonal. We checked.

A SHORT HISTORY OF DISTILLING IN ULSTER

Geographically, the province of Ulster comprises all of Northern Ireland plus three more counties: Donegal, Cavan, and Monaghan. It's the only region to rival—let alone even surpass—Dublin in terms of both volume and quality of the Irish whiskey it once produced (both licit and otherwise). In its nineteenth-century glory days, Royal Irish in Belfast was producing 2.5 million gallons of whiskey a year. What's more, the North's big distilleries found ready and thirsty markets for everything they could produce—at home and overseas.

At the time, Belfast, the regional capital, was a true Victorian powerhouse of heavy industry: engineering, manufacturing, and, of course, shipbuilding. It thrived on innovation. So while the great names of Dublin and Cork distilling scorned Aeneas Coffey's column still invention, Royal Irish, Avoniel, and Dunville in Belfast (and Watts in Derry, original producer of the legendary Tyrconnell) all said "yes, please." This decision triggered a further shift in production northward.

Beyond the distilling industry in Belfast and the bigger towns, there remained of course the colossus of the Causeway, Bushmills. Even setting aside the distillery's much-vaunted date of 1608, there's clear evidence of distilling in the area and in the wider Glens of Antrim going back much, much further. The Bushmills story is something of a soap opera in itself, at least until the late 1970s or so, when the cliffhangers finally ended and a lasting stability took hold, sort of.

Then there's Donegal. In the remote Inishowen Peninsula alone, for example, there were estimated to be some eight hundred *poitín* stills running in the nineteenth century. Think about that for a second. We're talking about a small part of a small county in a small country. You've got to admire that kind of dedication. However, by the early decades of the twentieth century, it had all but died out, even the moonshine. Coleraine Distillery staggered on, producing grain whiskey until the 1970s, and then that was it. Bushmills's were the last stills standing, as it were, and even they were looking a bit wobbly.

How things have changed. Today, a new generation of distillers is at work, helping to revive Ulster's whiskey-making history, and forge their own paths, as well, with new approaches, techniques, and ideas. But one thing they have in common is respect for the past. If Bushmills represents continuity, heritage, and reputation, the new makers, like Echlinville, are the torchbearers. And the future is looking very well illuminated indeed.

ULSTER
DISTILLERIES
OF TODAY

*The barrel hoops are building
up: The coopers are busier
than ever . . .*

THE OLD BUSHMILLS DISTILLERY

HERE WE ARE AT WHAT IS UNQUESTIONABLY THE JEWEL IN THE CROWN OF ULSTER DISTILLING. NOW, GIVEN ITS FAMOUS LONGEVITY, IT WOULD BE EASY TO ASSUME THAT WE ALL KNOW BUSHMILLS. IT'S THE QUIET, SOLID, STEADY ONE OF IRISH WHISKEY, RIGHT? THE ONE THAT JUST GETS ON WITH THE BUSINESS OF PRODUCING SOME OF THE FINEST *UISCE BEATHA* IN THE WORLD, JUST AS IT HAS FOR CENTURIES.

2 Distillery Road
Bushmills
County Antrim

www.bushmills.com

THE PROVINCE OF
ULSTER

Easy, yes, but a big mistake. The Bushmills story is a rollercoaster ride full of madcap twists and turns, colorful figures of questionable character, myriad changes of ownership, soaring heights, and near-calamities (some the work of fate, some largely self-inflicted). Yet through it all, its whiskeys have continued to garner fame and accolades the world over, and the distillery annually draws well over one hundred thousand visitors curious to learn the mystery behind the magic.

Let's start with the age question. And here's the thing: There may have been a little license with the license. It is true that a royal permit to distill was granted by King James I to a local landowner waaay back in 1608. But to this very spot? Well . . . That said, there's no denying that there's hundreds of years of distilling tradition up here on the wild and beautiful Causeway Coast. The original distillery was built in 1784 (when the pot still symbol seen on every label was first registered as a trademark). Today's distillery

Oh, the stories these stills could tell . . .

stands on the same spot, still fed by the same water source—St. Columb's Rill, a tributary of the River Bush.

Bushmills is one of the few distilleries in Ireland to use 100 percent unpeated malt barley. And one of even fewer that exclusively triple-distill their whiskey. Here, they maintain that's the source of Bushmills's distinctive, characteristic smoothness. The distillery has remained committed to small-batch production, with just ten copper pot stills at work around the clock. It's a true grain-to-glass operation, with every part of the process managed on-site, from mashing to distillation, warehousing, and bottling—all overseen by master distiller Colum Egan and master blender Helen Mulholland, the first woman to hold this role in the history of Irish distilling.

Famously, Bushmills was one of the earliest to make single malt as well as blended Irish whiskey. Both its celebrated Original and Black Bush are blends, though in the case of Black Bush, with an exceptionally high percentage of single malt (70 percent). The malt, of course, is pure Bushmills; the grain isn't. ("We don't make grain whiskey. We just make it better," goes the old joke around here.)

They're now up to twenty-three warehouses on-site, with plans to double that over the next couple of years. When you visit, you may notice that the warehouse numbers begin at seven. The first six aren't missing. It's a relic of the time when the Customs and Excise officers were resident there. The warehouses numbered one to six are actually inside the distillery, and relate to mashing, fermenting, and distilling. Just another example of the inherent eccentricity of the place.

Those warehouses (the actual ones) are currently home to around a quarter of a million casks. That's a lot of barrels. Luckily, there are generations of expert coopers to take care of them. In fact, there are generations of experts at work in many parts of the distillery. And that continuity, that history, is something they're very proud of here.

For all its prestige and renown, Bushmills is not a business resting on its laurels. It never has been. On the surface it may be a venerable institution, but underneath it's unusually sprightly—always innovating and exploring its capacity to

A fraction of a fraction of a fraction of all the casks in Bushmills's many warehouses.

surprise, experimenting with casks, malts, aging, and finishes. Some of these experiments will never see the light of day. But with Bushmills, you just never know what's coming next.

As they like to say around here, "You don't get to be the best because you're the oldest. You get to be the oldest because you're the best." And there's no disputing that, because one should never argue with one's elders—and betters.

AT A GLANCE

FIRST DISTILLATION
1784

STILLS
10 Pot Stills (Four Wash Stills 14,920L, Six Intermediate/ Spirit Stills 10,456L)

LPA
6 million, new stillhouse to double capacity

WHISKEY STYLES
Single Malt

VISITOR CENTER/TOURS
Yes

KEY BOTTLINGS

BUSHMILLS ORIGINAL
ABV: 40%

BLACK BUSH
ABV: 40%

BUSHMILLS 10
ABV: 40%

BUSHMILLS 16
ABV: 40%

BUSHMILLS 21
ABV: 40%

217

THE ECHLINVILLE DISTILLERY

SOMETIMES YOU CARRY AN IDEA AROUND WITH YOU FOR YEARS, NURTURING IT IN PRIVATE, DREAMING OF THE DAY WHEN YOU CAN BRING IT FORTH INTO THE LIGHT AND SET IT FREE. AND SOMETIMES THE IDEA JUST FINDS YOU, AND WON'T LET GO.

Echlinville House
62 Gransha Road
Newtownards
County Down

www.echlinville.com

THE PROVINCE OF
ULSTER

The latter is what happened with Echlinville founder Shane Braniff. He grew up here in the picturesque Ards Peninsula and even spent much of his early years in a pub owned by the family. But it didn't foster in him a love for the industry or for alcohol; quite the opposite. He went off and did other things in life: found a trade, started his own business, grew it, sold it, started another, grew it, etc. And then that old pub came up for sale. He bought it to bring it back into family ownership. That's all. It was a whim, he acknowledges; nothing but a sentimental whim. But then the idea came. The whiskey idea.

First, he created the Feckin and Strangford Gold brands, which he still owns. And then in 2013 he bought the majestic and historic Echlinville estate, which now includes a state-of-the-art still-house and the first license to distill spirits granted in Northern Ireland in over 130 years.

This is a condensed version of the timeline, because another thing

Echlinville's stills are creating new whiskeys—and reviving lost classics of Ulster distilling.

Shane has learned is that whiskey time is different. "In this industry we play the long game. We think not in terms of five, ten, or twenty years, but a hundred."

Part of this comes from generations of attachment to the land—this land—and an appreciation of terroir. Echlinville's barley is grown in the fields around the estate, malted here, distilled here. It's a true field-to-glass spirit.

The malting itself is special, too—a return to the old method in which the barley is thickly strewn over the floor and raked by hand. It's slow and labor-intensive but effective. And it's another indication of how things are done here. They take as long as they need; no corners are cut. That's because Shane's ambitions for the Echlinville brand are sky-high.

"We want to be recognized as the Irish Macallan. Nothing else will please me. We won't put our whiskey out until it's perfect. It's been aging for almost five years now. We are very pleased with how it's maturing, but we won't be releasing it until we're sure it's ready."

This distillery isn't just about the new brand. They're also reviving a lost classic of Irish whiskey. Today, Three Crowns, a peated blend and a twelve-year-old single malt, bear the once-illustrious Dunville's name again after nearly ninety years. The latest release from the brand is a seventeen-year-old single malt, finished in very rare forty-year-old ex-Demerara rum casks from the Port Mourant distillery in East Guyana, where their liquor is made in a wooden still. The whiskey already has two major accolades under its belt, having been named Best Irish Single Cask at the World Whiskies Awards and featured in Jim Murray's *Whisky Bible* (both 2018). Shane describes the revival of this once-great Belfast label as one of the founding goals of his venture. (In another nice design touch, look closely and you'll see that the crowns featured on the label are made up of stills.)

The distillery also produces a traditional white Irish whiskey, Bán Poitín, as well as the popular Jawbox Belfast Gin, and Echlinville, Ireland's first super-premium single-

The best of both: Echlinville combines leading-edge distilling with age-old traditions and techniques.

estate gin, which uses that homegrown, floor-malted barley.

The maturation warehouse has a traditional earthen floor, and the barrels are stored "on the bilge"— on their sides in order to maximize contact with the seasoned wooden staves. Again, not cheaper or more convenient, just better for the end product, Shane and master distiller Graeme Millar believe.

The distillery has plans for a visitor center and museum. Its regular tours include a personal greeting in the ballroom of the Echlinville manor house, an overview of the process from field to maturation warehouse, and tastings to finish.

For all its traditional values, Echlinville does not consider itself a craft distiller. The setup was designed to be scalable—as flexible as possible and as big as possible. It's a measure of the ambition behind the place. And they're in no hurry. They understand these things take time.

AT A GLANCE

FIRST DISTILLATION
2013

STILLS
2 Pot Stills; 2 Column Stills

WHISKEY STYLES
Single Malt, Pot Still & Grain

VISITOR CENTER/TOURS
Yes

KEY BOTTLINGS

DUNVILLE THREE CROWNS PEATED
ABV: 43.5%

DUNVILLE THREE CROWNS VINTAGE BLEND
ABV: 46%

DUNVILLE PX CASK SINGLE MALT
ABV: 46%

ULSTER *DISTILLERIES OF TODAY*

ULSTER'S GREAT IRISH PUBS

A snug in the exquisite Crown Bar in Belfast.

BRENNAN'S

Main Street
Bundoran
County Donegal

THE PROVINCE OF
ULSTER

TRISHA BRENNAN KEEPS HER PUB SPOTLESS. THE
FLOORS, TABLES, COUNTERS, GLASSES, PUMPS, AND
EVERY ONE OF THOSE FANTASTIC OLD MIRRORS ARE
POSITIVELY GLEAMING. IT'S THE WAY SHE WAS RAISED—
RIGHT HERE IN THIS VERY BUILDING, WHERE SHE STILL
LIVES TODAY.

BRENNAN'S

She's been working in the family bar for some fifty-five years now, and she spent her childhood around the place. Her affection for it is evident everywhere, and perhaps that's what makes it unique. As Trisha says, "Well, if you didn't love it and enjoy it, you wouldn't do it."

That's something that many of the publicans we met in the course of working on this book have said to us, as well. You see, some people have the notion that running a pub would be a laugh all the livelong day. It isn't. It's hard, hard work. There are many easier and certainly more lucrative ways to make a living. But if you love what you do . . .

This immaculate gem of a traditional Irish bar first opened

its doors on St. Patrick's Day in 1900. It hasn't changed much since then. There's central heating now and they changed the wallpaper "awhile back" and, well, that's about it.

They don't have a TV in Brennan's. Never have, never will. Somewhat unusually, there's no music or singing allowed either. People come for the conversation and the *craic*. "That's plenty enough for anyone," says Trisha, and who's going to argue with her?

The pub has always been popular with locals, of course, as well as tourists. These days, they're often joined by groups of surfers chasing the waves off Bundoran's coast. It all makes for a lively mix, "which is just the way it should be. Isn't that so?"

It is indeed, Trisha. It is indeed.

Her life's work: Trisha Brennan's immaculate pub.

Meet the boss.

NANCY'S

Front Street
Ardara
County Donegal

ARDARA WAS ONCE THE CENTER OF THE DONEGAL TWEED INDUSTRY. THAT MIGHT EXPLAIN WHY SOME OF THE TABLES IN NANCY'S USED TO HOUSE SEWING MACHINES. THEN AGAIN, MAYBE IT'S JUST COINCIDENCE. BECAUSE THE THING ABOUT NANCY'S IS, EVERYTHING ABOUT IT FEELS LIKE IT BELONGS THERE AND NOWHERE ELSE. PRETTY SOON, YOU WILL, TOO.

Nancy's is famous for two things: its seafood, which is brought in fresh every morning, and its hospitality. The latter is entirely due to the seven generations of the McHugh family who have stood behind the bar here to date. (And it's entirely possible that in due course another seven will, as well.) Today, owner Charlie still keeps an eye on things, while his son and daughter run the bar, and another son manages the kitchen (oysters are a real specialty here). Other children, siblings, and members of the extended family often help out about the place, too.

There are many imitation Irish pubs in this world, all leprechauns and diddly-dee, but there's no mistaking the real thing when you find it. And here it is. A former Irish Pub of the Year, Nancy's is a warren of small, cozy rooms, each one as homey and inviting as the next, which all adds up to plenty of opportunity to get lost.

So if you're traveling the Wild Atlantic Way, visit Ardara and stop at Nancy's. Treat yourself to a great pint of Guinness or an Irish Coffee, one of the craft beers or ciders they have on tap, or maybe sample some of the Irish whiskeys or gins lining the shelves. Have something to eat. Make yourself comfortable. Tell your best stories and you'll probably hear even better ones. Tomorrow can wait. The Wild Atlantic Way isn't going anywhere. And for now, if you're lucky, neither are you.

Yes, it's an old sewing machine table.

The back room is as cozy and quaint as a tea shop, but without the tea. Or the shop.

THE HOUSE OF McDONNELL

71 Castle Street
Ballycastle
County Antrim

THE PROVINCE OF
ULSTER

EILEEN AND THOMAS O'NEILL HAVE BEEN RUNNING THE
FAMILY PUB FOR AROUND FORTY YEARS, WHICH SOUNDS
LIKE A LONG TIME. BUT IT'S REALLY JUST A DROP IN
THE OCEAN. BECAUSE THIS PUB HAS BEEN IN THOMAS'S
FAMILY CONTINUALLY SINCE 1766. (THE McDONNELL
NAME COMES FROM HIS MOTHER'S SIDE.)

No other pub in Ireland has been in the same family as long. It's changed a bit since then, of course. In fact, it was refurbished as recently as, well, the mid-nineteenth century. And give or take a few light fittings, a cooler, and some new (ish) beer taps since, that's about as up-to-date as it gets.

It's a protected building, both inside and out, which is rare—and completely appropriate. The interior of this pub is stunning, with an amazing collection of antique distillers' mirrors and signs advertising long-forgotten goods.

The pub was a spirit grocer until Partition—the separation of Ireland into North and South in 1921. After this, as Eileen tells it, Thomas's grandfather, who was running the place then, was no longer legally able to operate two businesses under the one roof, the grocery and the pub. So he had to choose one to keep and one to close. He chose well.

(The old man was also the local vet, and farmers would regularly call in to consult him on livestock—and, of course, wet their whistle at the same time. No one seems to have bothered much about this instance of running two businesses in the same premises. But then of course, it wasn't the cattle's fault.)

Tom's, as it's affectionately known in the town, now finds itself serving second and third generations of the same families of customers. That said, business is slower these days. The pub really only opens regularly on Fridays—for its famous traditional music sessions, which attract some of the finest players in the country. ("It's mostly instrumental," says one regular, "but you'll always get great respect if you want to give a song.")

There's no TV and no food. But sure you can get those anywhere and any day of the week. Whereas here the pints are mighty and the *craic* is ninety—its highest measure. And you'll have to go a long way to find that on a Friday night, or any night for that matter.

The pub has been in the same family for over 250 years, and served generations of the same customers' families.

It's a protected building, both inside and out, which is rare...

JOHNNY JOE McCOLLAM'S

23 Mill Street
Cushendall
County Antrim

www.johnnyjoes.co.uk

**BEFORE THERE WAS ELECTRICITY HERE,
BEFORE THE TELEPHONE, THE CAR;
BEFORE THERE WAS EVEN A TOWN HERE,
THERE WAS THIS PUB.**

THE PROVINCE OF
ULSTER

Joe McCollam, custodian and keeper of the flame.

McCollam's, known locally as Johnny Joe's, has been on this beautiful spot since the 1830s. It's a style of bar that's increasingly rare in Ireland nowadays: the house pub. When you step in, you actually feel like you're in someone's home. And pretty soon, you'll come to think maybe it's your home. It's that kind of place, where you're instantly comfortable. In room after room (even the kitchen), there are people enjoying the *craic* and the open turf fires. And there's something else here: music, always music.

Not many pubs still have a piano in them these days. Johnny Joe's has two. That's an indication of the thing that makes this a very special pub indeed.

In McCollam's—a Traditional Music Pub of the Year—*seisiúns* just materialize. There's no structure or schedule. Instruments appear, musicians arrive from far and near, and then some more. It might be a couple, it could be thirty. You just never know.

A small pub with room for everyone. That's quite a trick.

In many ways, this is old Ireland here; very old. So if you're lucky, you might catch some *sean nós* singing—the ancient unaccompanied and highly ornamented Irish-language style. Perhaps someone will start to play an air, or there'll be some solo dancing, or a recitation, or all of the above. However, what you won't find here is any TV, radio, Wi-Fi, pool table, or gaming machine. (The very idea!)

> *So if you're lucky, you might catch some sean nós singing . . .*

As you'd expect, they serve a very fine pint here, and the whiskey and spirit selections are impressive, too. There's no food downstairs, but upstairs is, well, Upstairs at Joe's—an excellent seafood bar and steakhouse.

Johnny Joe's is run by the affable Joe McCollam and his wife, Sheila. However, he says modestly, "the ownership is really the community of customers we have. They make the place." We think there must be some kind of extra Glens of Antrim mojo involved, as well. There's just no other explanation.

FRANK OWENS

50 Main Street
Limavady
County Derry

WHEN YOUR FAMILY HOME IS ALSO A PUB, CERTAIN THINGS DON'T REALLY STRIKE YOU AS UNUSUAL, UNTIL THEY'RE POINTED OUT. LIKE THE SIGHT OF YOUR MOTHER BEHIND THE BAR DOING THE IRONING BEFORE OPENING UP. "THAT'S JUST THE WAY IT WAS," RECALLS DAMIAN OWENS, WHO NOW RUNS THE PUB HE GREW UP IN.

THE PROVINCE OF
ULSTER

The Game of Thrones *door panel: "It's not wood, you know; it's a magnet."*

That color scheme remind you of anything? Mine's a pint.

Back then, he and his siblings all had jobs to do about the place after school. In the days before beer taps, the main task was bottling the draft Guinness from the barrel. Dozens upon dozens of bottles of the black stuff filled—and labeled— by hand.

Of course, things are different now, and yet somehow the same. Because this pub still feels like a home, and almost makes you feel part of this extended family. That's a rare quality, and one to be cherished.

As far as our Great Irish Pubs go, this one is actually something of a whippersnapper, the building dating back only to 1929. It looks very much the same now as it must have then. It's a warm and comforting place, with a plain wooden floor and simple tables and stools. Around the walls there are some sports memorabilia—mostly GAA, golf, and rugby.

They keep things simple in Frank Owens. Simple and sublime.

One significant addition, however, arrived last year in the form of a door. A most remarkable carved door, depicting a scene from *Game of Thrones*. It was fashioned from a fallen tree in the Dark Hedges—the mysterious avenue of ancient beech trees outside Ballymoney that is a prominent location in the blockbuster show (which is partly filmed in Northern Ireland). As Damian discovered, his pub's presence on the increasingly busy *Game of Thrones* tourist trail has brought visitors from all over the world. He says of the door, "It's not wood, you know; it's a magnet."

Despite this brush with fantasy and fame, Frank Owens remains a resolutely traditional pub—known as "a good Guinness house," with an excellent whiskey selection (over 150 bottles), and a genuine, warm reception for all.

When Frank himself died in 2016, aged 99, Limavady was said to experience the nearest thing to a state funeral it had ever seen, such was the high regard in which he was held. But Frank left a fine legacy. You can visit it for yourself at 50 Main Street. It'll do your heart good.

THE CROSSKEYS INN

40 Grange Road
Toomebridge
County Antrim

www.crosskeys-inn.com

ONCE IN A WHILE YOU'LL FIND A PUB THAT'S SO SPECIAL, YOU'RE TEMPTED TO KEEP IT ALL TO YOURSELF. AND AS A RULE, WE'RE BIG FANS OF TEMPTATION. SO IT IS WITH SOME RELUCTANCE THAT WE GIVE YOU THE CROSSKEYS INN. BECAUSE IT'S JUST POSSIBLE THAT THIS PUB MAY BE PERFECT.

THE PROVINCE OF
ULSTER

For a start, we're talking about Ireland's oldest thatched pub, a cottage dating back well over three hundred years. The distinctive L-shaped building has at various times been "a dwelling house," a coaching inn, a post office, and a spirit grocer. Today it is a sublime pub and noted ceili house, with traditional musicians traveling from all over Ireland to play here for set dances and general diversion.

The name is thought to have been derived from the papal insignia of two crossed keys, the image of which once hung over the door.

When the current owner, Vincent Hurl, bought the Crosskeys in 2001, the pub had been closed for a time after a fire. Restoration went slower than Vincent expected, "but that's just the way it was," he says

matter-of-factly. He returned the exterior and interior to their original whitewashed state. The thatch was, of course, skillfully replaced. Inside, the original floors are still there, worn smooth and a bit uneven with the years, and the ceilings are surprisingly low (you'll learn that pretty quickly). There are old photographs and memorabilia everywhere—all with a story to match—and there's always a big open fire going.

Vincent is an enthusiastic pioneer of whiskey tourism, and consequently stocks a particularly fine range. He's ambitious for the place and has plans to add formal dining facilities and perhaps even accommodation. The Crosskeys doesn't offer food at present, except for large parties by arrangement. Menu options include the Eel Supper, a local Lough Neagh delicacy that's not to be missed— like The Crosskeys itself.

*Pretty as a picture:
Ireland's oldest
thatched pub.*

*Today it is a
sublime pub and
noted ceili house . . .*

*Take your seat;
things are about
to get lively.*

CROWN AND SHAMROCK INN

584 Antrim Road
Newtownabbey
County Antrim

www.crownandshamrock.co.uk

MOST OLD PUBS HAVE TALES, GHOST STORIES, AND MEMORIES APLENTY. NOT MANY OF THEM HAVE A SECRET ROOM. THE CROWN AND SHAMROCK DOES. AND IT WAS ONLY DISCOVERED BY CHANCE, WHEN THE BUILDING WAS BEING REWIRED IN THE 1950s.

THE PROVINCE OF
ULSTER

In the room were found old papers—and swords. Highwaymen's swords. Over a century before, this had been a halfway house for thirsty coachmen and miscellaneous ne'er-do-wells. It was a dangerous, rough-and-tumble place then—far removed from the wonderfully welcoming, traditional, family-run pub of today.

That warm welcome is due in large measure to Frances and Rosemary, sisters who grew up on the premises and who run it together. They know most of their customers by name, and they wouldn't have it any other way. They remember a time when the pub would be so packed on a Saturday night that customers simply filled every room of the house—the back kitchen, the living quarters, everywhere. Nobody

Everything about the place says "Welcome."

minded: That was just the Irish tradition of hospitality. And it's still here today.

The Crown and Shamrock—named in the late 1920s to reflect the twin traditions in the North—serves a very fine pint of Guinness, quite a few craft beers, and offers a good selection of gins and Irish whiskeys. It's also known for another thing: its fantastic traditional *seisiún* every Wednesday. If you get a chance to catch it, do. Grab it with both hands.

You'll find this lovely pub on the way to— or from—Belfast International Airport. As with John Kavanagh's (a.k.a. The Gravedigger's) in Dublin, many people stop in for a quick one on their way out of the country, then make it their first port of call on their return. It's easy to see why. It's an authentic taste of home—and sometimes nothing else will do.

Once a halfway house for thirsty coachmen and miscellaneous ne'er-do-wells . . .

THE GARRICK

29 Chichester Street
Belfast BT1

www.thegarrickbar.com

"KEEP IT SIMPLE, BUT MAKE IT THE VERY BEST YOU CAN." COLM OATES'S PHILOSOPHY ON WHAT MAKES A SUCCESSFUL PUB IS A GOOD ONE. AND A MUCH MORE COMPLICATED CHESS GAME THAN IT SOUNDS. FOR A START, STANDARDS HAVE TO BE SET VERY HIGH AND CONSISTENTLY MET.

THE PROVINCE OF
ULSTER

THE GARRICK

But, as manager of The Garrick, one of the city's oldest and most beloved establishments, a pearl of Belfast pubdom, Colm's clearly on to something.

There's been a tavern on this spot for well over a century. (It's said that originally it was a builders' yard that also went in for a little under-the-counter *poitín* trade. In due course, the liquor took over from the lumber.)

Today, The Garrick is a beautiful, warm, and inviting Victorian pub, with a trick or two up its elegant vintage sleeves. For a start, if you're into beer, this really is the place for you. At present, they have over ninety different bottled brands, as well as a cask ale offering (one of the very few in the city). In addition, there are over twenty gins and more than forty Irish whiskeys on those highly polished shelves. And if you just want a pint of Guinness and a half 'un, you're in luck here, too.

Music is big at The Garrick—there are three traditional sessions a week, plus a monthly unaccompanied singers' session upstairs, as well as regular DJ nights. Sport is popular, too, especially GAA, football (the other one), and rugby (the other other one). The food is good, as well—very high-quality pub food, heavy on premium local ingredients.

The Garrick is the kind of place that staff from other pubs turn to after their shifts. Because they recognize a good thing when they see it: great atmosphere, great service, and great drinks. Check and mate, Mr. Oates.

The Garrick: a true pearl of Belfast pubdom.

Today,
The Garrick
is a beautiful,
warm, and
inviting
Victorian pub...

THE DUKE OF YORK

7-11 Commercial Court
Belfast BT1

www.dukeofyorkbelfast.com

SOME PUBS MANAGE TO BE GREATER THAN THE
SUM OF THEIR PARTS. THE DUKE OF YORK IS
ONE OF THEM. AND GIVEN THAT THIS PUB IS
COMPOSED OF THOUSANDS UPON THOUSANDS OF
PARTS, THAT SHOULD GIVE SOME IDEA OF ITS
UNDENIABLE GREATNESS.

THE PROVINCE OF
ULSTER

At the center of this Belfast landmark is another, its legendary owner, Willie Jack: part philosopher, part entrepreneur, part raconteur, and all publican.

Willie's passion and enthusiasm for both his city and whiskey are boundless. (He also owns Ireland's sole whiskey-only emporium, the amazing Friend At Hand on nearby Hill Street. It's a definite must-see, if only to marvel at the vast collection of rare, unique, and special bottlings, including those in the cabinet marked "Never, Never, Never For Sale." But ask anyway.)

The pub Willie has created is a testament to his twin obsessions—as seen in the extraordinary collection of locally made artifacts and antique distillers' mirrors around the place. It's an extravagant style that one wag has called "Belfast baroque." (In fact, it was also the inspiration for The Dead Rabbit's own Taproom.)

The Duke, a real aristocrat among the city's pubs.

There'd been an inn of some sort here for over two hundred years before Willie Jack got his hands on it in the 1980s and began creating the extraordinary confection it is today. It's Belfast through and through; and that means it's also seen its fair share of history. Gerry Adams was a barman here in the 1970s. During The Troubles, the pub was actually blown up (by mistake apparently and, Willie insists, in no way a comment on the beer). It was painstakingly rebuilt. Many bands got their first break here, and live music is still a big part of The Duke's personality.

At heart, this is still a simple, no-nonsense pub. They've even painted their advice to customers outside: "Come in Soberly, Drink Moderately, Depart Quietly, and Call Again." There's no food here, except for Irish crisps and dulse, the equally feared and adored local dried seaweed delicacy. No cocktails, no alcopops. Just a great pint, a fantastic selection of whiskeys, and that frankly astonishing decor (complete with Yeats's "A Cradle Song" lettered on the staircase). Oh, and best of all, a genuinely warm atmosphere and a welcome for everyone. Because that's the thing about The Duke: He's a real gent.

MADDENS BAR

74 Berry Street
Belfast BT1

THE PROVINCE OF
ULSTER

MADDENS ISN'T GLAMOROUS AND IT'S CERTAINLY NO ARCHITECTURAL GEM. IT'S NOT PARTICULARLY ASSOCIATED WITH FAMOUS WRITERS OR HISTORICAL EVENTS, THOUGH IT'S SEEN PLENTY OF BOTH.

I t's well-worn, quite small, a bit rough around the edges, and, as your Irish granny might say, "a bit through-other" and higgledy-piggledy, its walls festooned with a million posters, flyers, signs, and cartoons. Oh, but it's got soul— Celtic soul—and by the bucketload.

There's traditional music played here seven nights a week, with a very popular Monday-night session where people just turn up and play. There are traditional set-dancing classes. Irish-language groups meet here. You see, in a city that can be a bit ambivalent about such things, Maddens wears its Irishness proudly. It also boasts that it serves the best Guinness in Belfast, which may very well be true.

The pub has been around since the mid-eighteenth century. It's changed hands a few times since then, although in fact surprisingly few. Today it's owned by Brian McMullan. He's kept it at its authentic Belfast best. There are no frills: just great pints, friendly staff and locals, plenty of banter, a big open fire, and, of course, there's the music.

True, at first the place may seem a bit random, but very quickly everything starts to make perfect sense. Trust us. In this city, Maddens is more than a pub. It's a true landmark—a place to seek out. Oh, and when you do, don't be put off by the two-way door system, which is an old security measure, a legacy of Belfast's troubled and dangerous past, when many pubs would screen who was coming in. It's not needed anymore. And in any case, with Maddens, once you're in, you just may never want to leave.

Famous for music, famous for pints, famous for the craic. That's plenty for anyone.

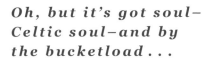

Oh, but it's got soul— Celtic soul—and by the bucketload...

KELLY'S CELLARS

30-32 Bank Street
Belfast BT1

www.kellyscellars.com

In Belfast, Kelly's is the secret we all know. If you grew up in the city, you've been here and heard a few stories. Maybe you even told a few yourself. Over the years, even through the worst of the bad times, it's been there for us.

THE PROVINCE OF
ULSTER

That's probably why we love it. It's the city's oldest licensed premises, dating back nearly three hundred years, and there's nothing fake or pretentious about the place, with its plain stone floor, alarmingly low ceilings, open fire, and whitewashed walls. It is what it is, just as it always has been. The sign outside reads *"Fáilte go Teach Uí Cheallaigh"*—"Welcome to Kelly's." And everyone truly is welcome here.

There are a couple of things that are genuinely special about this pub. Firstly, the music. It's always been a home away from home for traditional musicians, with sessions and gigs six days a week. Secondly, the Irish language (not as readily found in Belfast as in, say, Connemara). The owner, the redoubtable Lily Mulholland, and many of her staff are native speakers, so if you have a *cúpla*

focal—a couple of words—this is a good place to try them out.

Lily was a customer and a fan of Kelly's long before she became the owner. "There's just something about the place," she beams—almost as if she's still slightly amazed to find herself in charge. (But this Lily is no shrinking violet, mind—she once chased a would-be robber out of her pub and pursued him through the streets in blind indignation at his effrontery.)

Kelly's is a truly historic Irish bar, steeped in tales of rebellion and revolution, as reflected among the mad array of bric-a-brac on the walls. It's not surprising therefore that Kelly's is also a talker's pub. So expect banter and *craic* along with a great pint of Guinness and the excellent Irish stew.

Go if you can. And if you can't, start planning to. Every visit feels like a homecoming, and there's nothing better than that, now, is there?

Kelly's is a truly historic Irish bar, steeped in tales of rebellion . . .

The Irish language is spoken here, celebrated here, written on the walls here . . .

THE CROWN BAR

THE VICTORIANS GET A BIT OF A RAW DEAL SOMETIMES. THEY'RE MISCAST AS UPTIGHT PARTY POOPERS, ALL VINEGAR AND THIN-LIPPED DISAPPROVAL. AND THEN YOU GET THIS—AN EXTRAVAGANT CELEBRATION OF EXCESS THAT'S VICTORIAN THROUGH TO THE VERY BONES OF ITS CORSET, DESIGNED TO IMPRESS, TO THRILL, AND TO DELIGHT. AND ALL IN THE NAME OF NOTHING BUT PLEASURE.

THE PROVINCE OF
ULSTER

THE CROWN BAR

Built in 1826, Belfast's original Railway Tavern became The Crown Saloon in 1849. It gained its remarkable interior in the 1880s, and has kept it ever since (even surviving a major restoration in the 1970s).

It's quite possibly the finest remaining example of a Victorian gin palace in the world. And in Belfast, they're very proud of it. Well, just take a look. Stained-glass windows, mosaic floors, multi-colored tiles, pineapples, griffins, lions, clowns, seashells: They're all here, along with yards of burnished brass and expanses of polished wood beneath a ruby-red ceiling.

And of course, let's not forget the signature feature of the place: the famous snugs, those discreet booths, perfect for assignations or simply for those who prefer to knock back their pints and gin away from prying eyes.

The Crown is also a place of contradictions. For all its dazzling, prodigal glamour, it's really a down-to-earth pub, with no pretensions whatsoever. Yes, celebrities are frequently seen here. But there's really only ever one star. The Crown specializes, naturally, in gin, as well as cask ales. And there's good pub grub fare, too. "Nothing fancy; we're still a pub," as manager Andy Moore explains. "That means no TV, no cocktails, no music, just conversation."

Directly facing The Europa—which became infamous as Europe's most-bombed hotel during The Troubles—The Crown has sustained more than its share of damage over the years. But each time, they just put the pieces back together and started anew. In a sense, that's the spirit of the city itself, only with added pineapples and griffins.

The "Belfast baroque" style of the world's finest gin palace. World, you're welcome.

Today, the Crown is owned by the National Trust—a recognition of its unique value as part of the city's heritage. There's simply nowhere else like it. Visit if you can, book a snug beforehand, and leave the door open. You never know who might join you—and what could transpire.

It's pretty spectacular on the outside, too.

Beats an evening with the minibar, doesn't it?

GARTLAN'S

5 Lower Main Street
Kingscourt
County Cavan

FOR OVER A CENTURY, GARTLAN'S WAS THE
ADORNMENT OF MAIN STREET IN KINGSCOURT—
A GENUINE IRISH THATCHED PUB SO PICTURE-
PERFECT THAT ITS IMAGE WAS SEEN ON POSTERS
AND POSTCARDS SENT OUT AROUND THE WORLD.
IT WAS FEATURED IN BOOKS, COMMERCIALS, AND
FILMS LIKE ALEX FEGAN'S LOVELY *THE IRISH PUB*.

THE PROVINCE OF
ULSTER

GARTLAN'S

However, in 2008 The Crash—the global economic downturn—happened. The Celtic Tiger lost its roar. The people stopped coming. Gartlan's had survived a century, but it couldn't survive all that. Last orders were called.

By 2013 it was a sad sight. The famous thatch was sprouting great lurid clumps of weeds and the paintwork had faded and peeled. The windows were boarded up. A sapling was growing over the door. The name was still visible, but only just.

Then one day, as local woman Sheila Smith was driving past the pub, she thought, "Hmmm, I wonder . . ." She spoke to her husband, Padraig, and he, too, began to wonder. Could they? Should they? Oh, yes indeed, they should.

It took a long time, but they got there. And, in a way, that's not the most remarkable thing about what Padraig and Sheila achieved.

Because when they finally reopened the pub, it wasn't a new Gartlan's. It was the old one.

Padraig and Sheila had painstakingly photographed, annotated, and documented everything in the abandoned pub. Then they took it all away, cleaned it, numbered it, and stored it. And when the time was right, they replaced every curio and knicknack, every photograph and quirky sign exactly where it had been. They repaired and repainted. They fixed the old potbellied stove. They rethatched the famous roof. They turned back the clock.

The people returned, and they have kept returning. Now, some pubs are reverent places, made for philosophizing and earnest contemplation. Some are a haven for the connoisseur. This is a pub for joy. Milestones are marked here: christenings, weddings, anniversaries, Mondays . . . whatever you've got. The music is back, too. There are sessions every Sunday and Thursday. And, well, any day somebody feels like giving a song or a tune. If there's no music happening, there's conversation,

The old spirit grocer paraphernalia is still on show.

which is much the same thing. (A sign behind the bar says, "No Wi-Fi Here—Talk To Each Other." And so people do.)

There's a TV, somewhere, but since it's never turned on, no one pays it any mind. There's no food on offer either. But the pints are mighty, and there's a fair selection of whiskeys, gins, and all manner of hooch.

Sheila Smith, savior of Gartlan's.

And don't let the thatched roof deceive you. Gartlan's isn't some theme pub trading on nostalgia. No, it's about traditional virtues of conviviality and hospitality. It's genuine, the authentic article—all over again.

COCKTAILS
AND EXTRAS

COCKTAILS

Here are some cocktails we've specially created for this book, each designed around the distinctive qualities of one of these outstanding Irish whiskeys. All the recipes are for one cocktail serving. But first, a mini master class of tips, tricks, and explanations.

TERMINOLOGY AND TECHNIQUES

METHODS

SHAKEN: Assemble the drink in the order of the recipe, using the larger part of a cocktail shaker. Add ice to the top of the shaker, cover with the smaller part, and then really go for it. You want the ice to swirl around in there, not just go up and down. You're trying to incorporate air here. If your drink comes out of the shaker with a nice frothy top, you've got what you were looking for. Tip: Pour the drink into your glass over fresh ice; don't use the ice in the shaker.

STIRRED: Here you'll assemble the drink—in the order of the recipe, of course—in a mixing glass or beaker, and ideally use a barspoon to stir. (It has a long, spiral handle that enables the spoon part to rotate freely in the drink like a propeller—doing all the work for you.) Ice is crucial to stirred drinks. The goal is to get the drink both cold and diluted down to a pleasant balance. Tip: Once you've stirred your drink, don't do a long, showboat pour; it adds bubbles to the drink, which you've been trying to remove with all that stirring.

BUILT: This is the simplest and fastest method of creating a cocktail. It involves adding one ingredient after another straight into the serving glass in the order directed by the recipe. There's no shaking or stirring involved. Built drinks are often long, and are generally served in a highball or Collins glass. Speaking of which . . .

GLASSWARE

Of course, you don't have to use the specific style of glass we recommend here. However, our recommendations aren't random: The right glass does enhance the overall experience of the cocktail. And there are good reasons for that—for example, the shape can determine the aromatic hit you get from the drink as you raise it to your lips.

HIGHBALL OR COLLINS: a tall, straight-sided glass, with a fairly narrow neck.

OLD-FASHIONED: a short, squat, heavy-bottomed tumbler with straight sides. Also known as a rocks glass.

COCKTAIL GLASS: Sometimes called a martini glass, this is the classic V-shaped one everyone knows. Usually has a stem.

NICK & NORA: a bell-shaped glass with a stem—a bit like an elongated wineglass.

IRISH COFFEE GLASS: We recommend our own special Dead Rabbit glass for this, our signature drink, but in any case, do use a relatively thick glass with a good stem (remember: the drink is hot!). In terms of size we recommend no more than a six-ounce volume.

ICE

Again, it's a detail, but one that matters. A single large rock will keep your drink cold and dilute it slower; more pieces means faster dilution. Which one you use depends on the style of the drink.

GARNISHES

Most of the garnishes used here are citrus twists cut from the skin of the fruit (without getting any of the white pith). The skin is where the aromatic oils are. We recommend holding a twist skin-side down and about five inches from the top of the glass. Pinch the twist and you'll release a spritz of aromatic loveliness over the surface of the drink. Don't rim the glass with the twist, just discard it. (And don't put it in the drink either, as it will continue to release oils, changing the flavor of the cocktail.) If the drink calls for nutmeg, be sure to use a proper nutmeg grater because it will produce the fine dusting the recipe needs. Never use the ground stuff: It's horrible in a cocktail.

A NOTE ABOUT INGREDIENTS

Some of the ingredients used in these cocktail recipes, such as the syrups, aren't available off-the-shelf. You have to make them. But don't worry, they're easy to do, they taste fantastic, and they'll keep in the refrigerator for two weeks. (Plus, you can also give yourself a little pat on the back afterward. Just don't spill your lovingly prepared cocktail when you do.)

SYRUPS

CANE
INGREDIENTS: 2 parts organic evaporated cane juice, 1 part water

METHOD: Cook the cane juice and water in a pot over medium heat and stir until the sugar is dissolved. Bring to a rolling boil and then remove from the heat. Cool and store in the refrigerator for up to 2 weeks.

COFFEE-CHICORY - MAKES HALF A LITER
INGREDIENTS: 8.5 ounces of black coffee, 1.1 pounds of sugar, 1 tablespoon ground chicory root

METHOD: Place the ingredients in a large pot and bring to a boil, stirring frequently. Remove from the heat, place in an airtight container, and let cool at room temperature for 1 hour. Pass through a fine-mesh strainer, then bottle and refrigerate.

DEMERARA
INGREDIENTS: 2 parts organic Demerara sugar to one part water

METHOD: Place the sugar and water in a pot and mix well. Heat at 175°F and continue to stir until the sugar is completely dissolved. Bring to a rolling boil, then remove from the heat. Cool, bottle, and refrigerate.

SIMPLE SYRUP
INGREDIENTS: 1 part sugar, 1 part water

METHOD: Combine the sugar and water in a saucepan over medium heat, stirring slowly until the sugar is dissolved. Transfer to an airtight container and let cool at room temperature. Bottle and refrigerate.

RICH HONEY
INGREDIENTS: 2 parts clover honey, 1 part water

METHOD: Soften all the honey in its container by placing it in a water bath. Then whisk with half as much fresh hot water. Bottle and refrigerate.

MARASCHINO LIQUEUR
This is a house blend we use, which is half dry kirsch eau-de-vie, half sweet cherry liqueur.

JUICES
Always freshly squeezed.

CIDER
Here, we're talking about dry or semidry alcoholic English apple cider. Nothing else will do.

TULLAMORE DISTILLERY

SHORT & SWEET

This is a twist on the classic Bajan Corn 'n' Oil cocktail. In the original, the dark rum floats on top of the whiskey (the "corn"), like a glistening slick of oil. Our version showcases the distinctive aromatic quality of the rum-casked whiskey, as well as its heavier alcohol content.

INGREDIENTS:

3 dashes Angostura bitters

1 teaspoon Cane Syrup (page 253)

1 teaspoon freshly squeezed lime juice

0.25 ounce Velvet Falernum

0.5 ounce Pierre Ferrand Dry Curaçao

2 ounces Tullamore D.E.W. Caribbean Rum Cask

METHOD:	Stirred
GLASSWARE:	Old-Fashioned
ICE:	Large Rock
GARNISH:	Orange Twist, discard

TULLAMORE DISTILLERY

GRINDSTONE

This is a lovely summery riff on the classic Stone Fence cocktail. The original dates back to the American Revolutionary War. The story goes that the night before the Green Mountain Boys attacked the British-held Fort Ticonderoga, they drank a mixture of rum and hard cider for courage. This version is altogether more peaceable, highlighting the whiskey's unusual cider cask finish.

INGREDIENTS:

2 dashes Boston Bittah's

0.75 ounce American Fruits Apple Liqueur

0.5 ounce Green Chartreuse

1.5 ounces Tullamore D.E.W. Cider Cask

4 ounces semidry cider

METHOD:	Built
GLASSWARE:	Highball
ICE:	Big Chunks
GARNISH:	Lemon Twist, discard

COOLEY DISTILLERY

WILD IRISH ROSE

Here, the smokiness of the Connemara Peated plays wonderfully off the sweet fruits and citrus notes of pomegranate and grapefruit.

INGREDIENTS:

1 egg white

2 dashes grapefruit bitters

0.75 ounce freshly squeezed lemon juice

0.75 ounce grenadine

0.5 ounce Aperol

1 ounce Laird's Bonded Applejack

1 ounce Connemara Peated Irish Whiskey

METHOD:	Shaken
GLASSWARE:	Cocktail Glass
GARNISH:	Grapefruit Twist, discard

TEELING DISTILLERY

AGAINST THE GRAIN

A riff on an old nineteenth-century cocktail called Red Cup, this version brings out the tannins and berry notes in the whiskey.

INGREDIENTS:

1.5 ounces Teeling Single Grain

0.5 ounce Graham's LBV Port Wine

0.5 ounce freshly squeezed lemon juice

0.5 ounce lemon sherbet

1 teaspoon red currant preserves

1.5 ounces dry cider

METHOD:	Shaken and Built
GLASSWARE:	Highball
GARNISH:	Seasonal Berries in Simple Syrup (page 253)

TEELING DISTILLERY

THUNDERBOLT

An Old-Fashioned built around this intensely aromatic whiskey. The rum note works particularly well with the banana and ginger.

INGREDIENTS:

2 dashes Angostura bitters

2 dashes Xocolatl Mole Bitters

0.25 ounce St. Elizabeth Pimento Dram

0.5 ounce Giffard Ginger Liqueur

0.5 ounce Giffard Crème de Banane

1.5 ounces Teeling Small Batch

METHOD:	Stirred
GLASSWARE:	Old-Fashioned
ICE:	Block
GARNISH:	Orange Twist, discard

THE DUBLIN LIBERTIES DISTILLERY

CIVIL SERVANT

The origins of the Chancellor cocktail are obscure: possibly Scottish, possibly not. No one's really sure, although it is certainly one of the earliest successful whiskey-based cocktails, akin to a Manhattan in style. Our version is more of a sour, the whiskey providing intensity and backbone against the classic coffee, port, and amaro combination.

INGREDIENTS:

2 dashes Jerry Thomas Decanter Bitters

½ teaspoon Demerara Syrup (page 253)

0.75 ounce freshly squeezed lemon juice

0.75 ounce Coffee-Chicory Syrup (page 253)

0.25 ounce Graham's LBV Port Wine

0.25 ounce Amaro di Angostura

1.5 ounces Dead Rabbit Irish Whiskey

METHOD:	Shaken
GLASSWARE:	Cocktail Glass
GARNISH:	Freshly Grated Nutmeg

MIDLETON DISTILLERY

CUSTOM MAID

The Maid is classically based on gin or vodka. Our version was created to let the grain and pot still elements of this special whiskey linger and shine. It is shaken with cucumber and then garnished with a slice to finish.

INGREDIENTS:

2 thin slices cucumber, unpeeled

0.75 ounce freshly squeezed lemon juice

0.75 ounce Simple Syrup (page 253)

0.5 ounce St. Germain Elderflower Liqueur

2 ounces Jameson Black Barrel

METHOD: Shaken

GLASSWARE: Old-Fashioned

ICE: Cracked Ice

MIDLETON DISTILLERY

TIPPERARY

This Manhattan-style drink is all about big, bold flavors, with the pot still whiskey to the fore against the Chartreuse and bitters.

INGREDIENTS:

2 dashes Angostura bitters

2 dashes orange bitters

2 dashes absinthe

0.5 ounce Green Chartreuse

1.5 ounce sweet vermouth

1.5 ounces Powers John's Lane

METHOD: Stirred

GLASSWARE: Nick & Nora

GARNISH: Orange Twist, discard

MIDLETON DISTILLERY

REVOLVER

This variation on an Old-Fashioned highlights Green Spot's distinctive light, floral, and crisp apple notes.

INGREDIENTS:

2 dashes Peychaud's Bitters

½ teaspoon Menthe Pastille

0.25 ounce Suze Gentiane

0.75 ounce Dolin Blanc

0.5 ounce Copper & Kings Un-Aged Apple Brandy

1.5 ounces Green Spot

METHOD:	Stirred
GLASSWARE:	Nick & Nora
GARNISH:	Lemon Twist, discard

MIDLETON DISTILLERY

CITY SLICKER

The spices and tannins in the Redbreast are complemented by sherry and sweet vermouth. Smooth and classy.

INGREDIENTS:

0.25 ounce Sommer Picon

0.25 ounce Maraschino Liqueur (page 253)

0.75 ounce Cocchi di Torino

1.5 ounces Redbreast Irish Whiskey 12-Year-Old

METHOD:	Stirred
GLASSWARE:	Nick & Nora
GARNISH:	Orange Twist, discard

BUSHMILLS DISTILLERY

GRASS ROOTS

A simple twist on the classic Collins, accentuating the crisp green apple, pear, and honey notes of the whiskey.

INGREDIENTS:

1.5 ounces Bushmills Single Malt 10-Year-Old

0.5 ounce Merlet Crème de Poire

0.5 ounce Pear Eau-de-Vie

0.75 ounce freshly squeezed lemon juice

0.5 ounce Rich Honey Syrup (page 253)

2 dashes absinthe

1.5 ounces soda water

METHOD:	Shaken and Built
GLASSWARE:	Highball
ICE:	Big Chunks

BUSHMILLS DISTILLERY

DEAD RABBIT IRISH COFFEE

Here it is, the legendary, world-beating version. Can it really be as good as they say? Oh, yes it can. Honestly.

INGREDIENTS:

1 ounce Bushmills Original

0.5 ounce Demerara Syrup (page 253)

3.5 ounces Dead Rabbit Blend Coffee—or other medium-dark roast—made in a French press

Thumb of prepared whipped cream

METHOD:	Built
GLASSWARE:	Irish Coffee Glass
GARNISH:	Freshly Grated Nutmeg, optional

GLOSSARY

This is by no means an exhaustive list of terms you may encounter while exploring the exceptional work of Irish distilleries and the equally fine work done in our pubs. Some of the references are technical and some are less serious but also useful to know, especially if you plan on conducting proper investigations in the land of uisce beatha.

ABV
Alcohol By Volume: a number indicating the strength or proof of the whiskey. By law, Irish whiskey must be a minimum of 40 percent ABV. Otherwise the cuffs go on.

Age Statement
A number usually found on the label of a whiskey bottle. It indicates the youngest whiskey used in the production of the bottle's contents.

Anadipsia
A ten-dollar word—meaning excessive thirst—that doesn't actually feature anywhere in this book, other than here. And yet, somehow, it pervades every page.

Angels' Share
There's a whimsical notion that this is the portion of the maturing whiskey that's simply lost to the ether. But let's just call it what it is: metaphysical larceny.

Ball of Malt
A measure of whiskey in licensed premises. May also be called "a half 'un."

Barred
Ejected from a pub on account of bad behavior with the explicit directive not to return. Often heard in Dublin anecdotes involving Brendan Behan, whose writing, he once remarked, tended to get in the way of his drinking.

Black Stuff, The
Guinness. Note: This term cannot be applied to any other stout. Hey, we don't make the rules.

Blend
Most Irish whiskey is a blend of pot still, grain, and/or single malt whiskey. This is where blending becomes an art form. Classics include Jameson, Tullamore D.E.W., Bushmills, and Powers.

Bodhrán
Pronounced bow-rawn, this is the ancient hand-held drum that features strongly in traditional Irish music. Requires great skill to play well, and none to play badly.

Bourbon Cask
Or more accurately, ex-bourbon cask (the bourbon has been thoughtfully removed). This is the preferred type of cask used for maturing whiskey. The bourbon seasons the wood just the way we like it.

Cask Strength
A number indicating that the whiskey was not diluted when it was taken from the barrel and bottled. This means it is higher proof—or stronger. You have been warned.

Ceili
A party of traditional Irish music and dancing. They tend to start rowdy and deteriorate from there.

Color
All whiskey is clear when it goes into the barrel for maturing. The type of wood used at this stage and at finishing will provide the color of the uisce beatha you later lovingly gaze upon in your glass.

Column Still
The other type of still. This is the whippersnapper of the distillation world, having been around for less than two hundred years. It produces a lighter, purer grain spirit with a weaker flavor but stronger ABV.

Cooper
A skilled maker and repairer of barrels and casks. A hugely important figure in any distillery.

Craic
The quintessential Irish word. It's hard to translate but easy to recognize. If you're having a good time in a pub, craic is present. It's a combination of fun, laughter, divilment, and diversion. It may also appear on a pub sign—"Craic Agus Ceol," which means "craic and music." Now that's a good sign.

Distillation
The mysterious process whereby grain, water, and yeast become uisce beatha. There's a lot of science around it, but to be honest, no one really knows how it works. Molecules? Magnets? Magic? Let's just go with magic.

Diversion
Primary meaning: a companion to craic. Only occasionally refers to traffic rerouting. After all, what's your rush?

Draw
The length of pipeline from a beer barrel to the tap. Really only ever discussed in relation to Guinness. Received wisdom insists the shorter the better. Received wisdom is correct.

Dunnage
See Rackhouse.

Fermentation
The wort is cooled and poured into a fermentation vessel (also called a washback). These are usually stainless steel, though you will find wooden ones in use. Yeast is then added and things get going as the sugars in the wort are converted into alcohol.

Finish
A tasting term to describe what happens immediately after you've taken a sip of whiskey as the flavors continue to develop on your palate, you lucky thing.

Finishing
After whiskey has matured for a number of years, usually in bourbon casks, it is often "finished" for a second, shorter period of time in a different type of cask. Seasoned ex-fortified wine barrels—sherry, port, Madeira, etc.—are popular, though distillers will often experiment with other types, such as rum and cognac, or chardonnay, Merlot, and Bordeaux wine barrels. Finishing delivers depth of flavor, and profoundly influences the aroma and color of the whiskey. It's clever stuff.

GAA
The Gaelic Athletic Association (GAA) is the governing body of Ireland's traditional sports: Gaelic football, hurling, camogie (women's hurling), etc.—and as such, the most important thing in the world, particularly on a Monday, since many games are played on Sundays.

Grain to Glass
This term describes a whiskey that has been produced using the distiller's own barley and own new-make spirit (see Sourced Whiskey). The entire process is controlled by the distiller. Clonakilty and Echlinville are good examples. Sometimes also called "farm to glass."

Grist
See Milling.

Heads
The earliest evaporations from the distillation process. These contain less desirable compounds, which the distiller uses the spirit still to identify, and then discard, usually with a snort of derision.

Heart
The middle section of the distillation sandwich— the good stuff, with none of the early unpleasant elements ("heads") or the later unpleasant ones ("tails").

Lauter Tun
A type of mash filter, sometimes called a mash tun. It works much like a large sieve, to separate solids from the mash.

Low Wines
The product of the first distillation in a pot still. Not as miserable as it sounds.

LPA
Stands for Liters Per Annum—a measure of the volume of whiskey produced by a distillery in a year. It's a more standard way of assessing output than the number of bottles or cases, both of which vary in size.

Madeira Drum
A fortified wine cask (approximately 650 liters) widely used for finishing mature whiskey. Possibly also a terrible band you secretly used to like in the eighties.

Malting
The process of tricking the barley into germinating, which triggers the production of enzymes. These in turn will convert the starch into the sugars needed by yeast for distillation. Yes, it's sneaky but necessary. And the barley gets over it.

Mashbill

The mixture of various grains used to make the wort. The what? No, the wort. Oh, OK, better include that one, as well.

Mash Filter

A technology more traditional in brewing than distilling, it separates the sugar solution from the malt solids. Midleton has one of these. Many distillers use a variation called a lauter tun.

Mashing

Here, the grist is mixed with warm water in a vessel called a mash tun. This triggers the conversion of starch to sugars, ready for exposure to yeast. The process is repeated two more times.

Milling

The process in which the malt is ground into a coarse, flour-like material called grist.

New-Make

Newly made spirit that's the basis of whiskey. Um, that's about it.

Nose

A tasting term used to describe the aroma of the whiskey. As a rule of nose, the bigger, the more complex the whiskey.

Peated

A style of whiskey more associated with Scotch. It is made with barley that has been peat-dried, which lends a distinctive smoky note. The most popular Irish peated whiskey is Kilbeggan's Connemara, though some of the new generation of distillers are also experimenting with the style. Those crazy kids.

Plain

See Black Stuff, The. Bonus Irish points if you quote Flann O'Brien's "The Workman's Friend" when using the term. (Key line: "A pint of plain is your only man.") Ah, sure you're one of us now.

Poitín

Sometimes spelled potcheen or poteen and pronounced "putcheen," it is the clear and ancient spirit—Irish moonshine. Many distilleries now produce it commercially and, yes, legally. Hurrah!

Port Pipe

The distinctive type of barrel in which port is matured. Once emptied of port, these make great gifts for distillers, as do sherry butts and rum casks. Hint, hint.

Pot Ale

This is the liquor left in the wash still after the first distillation. It is protein-rich and distilleries often pass it on to local farmers for use in animal feed (along with the dry residue called draff). And no, it doesn't get them drunk. We checked.

Pot Still

The oldest form of still used in Irish whiskey-making. It has a distinctive bulb or dome shape that goes back to the alembics that monks first used to distill medicine and fragrances in the medieval era. The term is also used to describe the superior traditional style of whiskey the still produces.

Rackhouse

Hello, did Dunnage send you? In a rackhouse, whiskey barrels were traditionally stored on their sides rather than upright. Some distillers maintain that this gives more contact between the whiskey and the seasoned cask wood, and that this helps develop flavor, which is almost certainly possibly maybe true.

Reflux

A technique by which spirit vapors are condensed and returned to the distillation chamber in order to purify them. More clever stuff.

Seisiún

Pronounced say-SHOON, this is a traditional Irish music session of airs, songs, and, ideally, rowdiness. They tend to be informal but respectful, and there is an etiquette involved: If you don't know the tune, don't busk it. One you know will be along eventually.

Shebeen

Illegal drinking den and forerunner of the licensed premises henceforth known unto humanity as the Irish pub.

Sherry Butt

Type of cask often used for finishing an aged whiskey. This one used to have—yes—sherry in it. (You're really getting the hang of this, aren't you?) The fortified wine lends color and flavor.

Single Grain

An Irish whiskey from one distillery. Can be produced using corn, wheat, and barley—with a small addition of malted barley for those useful enzymes. Typically made in a column still.

Single Malt

An Irish whiskey made using only malted barley.

Single Pot Still

A style of whiskey only legally made in Ireland (and therefore the best, so there). It is produced in a pot still—of course—at a single distillery using both malted and unmalted barley.

Sláinte

How to say "cheers" in Irish. It's a wish for good health to all, and is pronounced slawn-cha. More bonus Irish points for you.

Snug

A private booth in a pub. These were once the preserve of women, whose presence on licensed premises was so alarming a man once nearly spilled a drink. He didn't, but it was a close thing. In later years, lots of horse-trading, cattle-trading, and even match-making went on in snugs. Oh, and drinking.

Sourced Whiskey

Whiskey takes time. When a distillery is just starting up, it doesn't have a supply of its own new-make let alone aged spirit, so it uses sourced whiskey supplied by another distiller, such as Great Northern.

Spirit Grocer

A peculiarly Irish enterprise that traditionally combined the services of both a grocer's shop and a pub under one roof. We've always taken a very practical view of the essentials of life.

Spirit Safe

This is a large, glass-walled box that sits within the distillation chain. It's crucial for allowing the distiller to assess the spirit coming out of the pot still, and deciding when to stop (or "cut") distillation. And yes, it's usually padlocked. Honestly, it's for its own good.

Still

This is the heart of the distillery, the apparatus in which the magic happens. There are two types used in whiskey-making: the pot still, which is shaped like a pot, and the column still, which is, well—you get the picture. The column still is sometimes called the Coffey still, after its inventor, Aeneas Coffey.

Tails

The later evaporations from the distillation process. These contain less desirable compounds, so the distiller will want to identify these in the spirit safe and discard them, with the same derision employed with the heads.

Teetotal

Eschews all alcoholic drinks. Perhaps surprisingly, some of the most prominent distillers and even great publicans are teetotal. For them, it's not about booze, it's about the business of hospitality.

Turf

Peat dried for fuel. Once very commonly used in rural Ireland to heat homes and pubs. Burns with a distinctive aroma that instantly induces homesickness in Irish people, even when they are at home.

Uisce Beatha

The Irish term that became anglicized (them again!) into whiskey. Also known as the pure drop. It's pronounced ISH-ka BAh-ha and means "the water of life." So you can see, we've always taken this stuff very seriously.

Warehouse

A crucial component in the whiskey process. This is where time really gets to work. The whiskey is in prolonged contact with the cask wood. Air is moving around the casks. (Some coastal distillers insist that the sea air definitely affects the flavor of their whiskey.) Here, friends, is where whiskey waits in casks that are either palletized and vertically stacked or laid horizontally on their side. In the latter case the warehouse is called a rackhouse, rickhouse, or dunnage. If a distillery were the United States, this would be its Fort Knox.

Wort

This is the liquid produced by the mashing process involving the malted barley. It contains all the sugars that the yeast will cleverly convert to alcohol.

INDEX

YOUR GUIDES

Meet the Team

SEAN MULDOON
Pub Expert

Sean is best known for The Dead Rabbit Grocery and Grog in Lower Manhattan— the bar he founded in 2012 with his business partner, Jack McGarry. Combining the best of traditional Irish pub hospitality with some of the world's best cocktails, The Dead Rabbit has won almost every major award in the industry, including "World's Best Bar" (twice).

Before moving to New York, Sean was bar and potation manager at the Merchant Hotel in his native Belfast, when it was named World's Best Cocktail Bar in 2010. In 2015 Sean and Jack collaborated with hospitality legend Danny Meyer in the creation of GreenRiver in Chicago, a restaurant and bar themed around the Irish presence in the history of the Second City.

In 2016 Sean and Jack opened their second venue in New York City. BlackTail is a Cuban-styled bar based around the post-Prohibition golden age of cocktails, a style they simply call "the lush life." Sean consults throughout the world on pubs, hospitality training and standards, and drinks menu creation.

JACK McGARRY
Mixed Drink Expert

Jack McGarry is The Dead Rabbit's cofounder and operating partner. He also created its extraordinary drinks program. In July 2013, he was named International Bartender of the Year at the prestigious Tales of the Cocktail awards. He is its youngest-ever recipient, and to date only the second in America.

To realize the Dead Rabbit project, Jack tested hundreds of mixed-drink recipes from the nineteenth century onward. Each recipe was adjusted to account for contemporary palates, and regularly involved fifty to seventy versions before one was considered just right. His resulting menu was a landmark in the industry, and confirmed Jack as a global authority.

TIM HERLIHY
Distillery Expert

Born and raised in County Louth, Tim began his working career at the iconic Cooley Distillery, learning the industry all the way from grain to glass.

As Tullamore D.E.W. ambassador, Tim is a frequent presenter at whiskey shows and cocktail weeks, discussing history, cocktails, and one of his favorite topics, the Irish pub. Preceding St. Patrick's Day 2014, Tim completed a twenty-eight-day lecture tour of the best Irish pubs in all fifty U.S. states, plus the District of Columbia. The achievement is still spoken of in whispered tones, mostly by Tim.

A natural raconteur and never at a loss for a toast, Tim has led television segments on *Access Hollywood Live, Fox and Friends,* and *The Steve Harvey Show,* among others. In 2016, he became *Whisky Magazine*'s Icons of Whisky award-winner for Irish Whiskey Brand Ambassador of the Year.

ELAINE HILL
Photographer

As Eve Arnold (more or less) said, the instrument is not the camera but the photographer. In other words, who you are shapes what you make.

Elaine's images say very strongly who she is: witty, insightful, meticulous, and creative. Based in Belfast, she works in areas from commercial and corporate projects to portraiture and the performing arts. But it is in the highly specialized field of food and beverage photography that Elaine has truly distinguished herself.

Over the past ten years, her images have helped reposition major spirit brands, launched cool restaurants (and some even cooler maverick chefs), gotten beneath the skin of the guarded, and found the beauty in the everyday. Yes, Elaine is friendly and approachable. But make no mistake: She's going to get that shot.

CONOR KELLY
Writer

Conor is like a tree: If you sliced through him, you'd
see rings of words. But please don't do that. (Blood
is so hard to get out of a laptop.) He is from a talky
Irish family where storytelling is a competitive and,
occasionally, full-contact sport. Over the years, he has
corralled words as a journalist, translator, copywriter,
and book editor—shaping manuscripts on everything from
instruction manuals and biographies to historical fiction
and university textbooks. More importantly, however, he
provides The Dead Rabbit's tone of voice and gets to write
the bar's extraordinary story-menus and promotional
materials. In the face of seemingly relentless peer
pressure, Conor nonetheless retains an abiding love for
the semicolon; like this one. What a lovely thing.

ACKNOWLEDGMENTS

There are many people who helped make this book possible. Firstly, we have to thank everyone who gave up their time to participate in our crazy project—especially the distillers and pub owners, and their friends, family, and staff. We're also particularly grateful to Kilbeggan Distillery for their kind permission to shoot the cocktail pics there.

Many thanks also to Rebekkah Dooley, who planned, organized, and coordinated the trips; and Jack McGarry Sr., who drove us the length and breadth of Ireland, twice. And of course, we mustn't forget Poppy, our Whiskey Boys on Tour VW van, who endured so, so much. (Forgive us, Poppy.)

To them and to everyone who came out to see us along the way, thank you all—and cheers!

Go raibh míle maith agaibh go léir—agus sláinte!